Praise

SALES ESSENTIALS

I've been building and leading sales teams for two-thirds of my existence, and I have a passion for learning. Rana Salman's *Sales Essentials* is a must-read for lifelong learners and those who genuinely want to invest in successful sales behaviors and techniques, and truly understand the sales process fundamentals. This book delivers the what, why, and how and is written to be shared. It is a foundational teaching platform for individual sellers and leaders to take a step-by-step journey with Rana, who shapes the narrative around the criticality of the "human connection," which is truly the basis for success!

> —**Brenda Hudson,** senior vice president of commercial sales,
> sales enablement, learning, and development, Insight

Rana Salman's *Sales Essentials* is not your typical sales book. Rana integrates her experience and passion for selling with science, real-life stories, research, and data. The book cuts through the fluff and provides practical applications and actionable insights on how to sell. It's not a sales book you read once and put away. It's a guide reps can regularly use throughout the sales process.

> —**Ben Brewer,** chief sales officer, Cornerstone OnDemand

Rana Salman's *Sales Essentials* is a comprehensive guide on how to sell and build profitable relationships. She doesn't hold back, sharing her experiences (the highs and the lows) and providing a succinct approach to selling in today's environment. The book includes tools, exercises, templates, and examples that any seller, no matter their tenure or background, can benefit from. I highly recommend this book!

> —**Rashim Mogha**, senior vice president and general manager of leadership and business portfolio, Skillsoft, and member, Forbes Business Council

Sales Essentials is incredibly relatable and current. It gives real-world examples and good reminders you can take into your daily practice. Rana Salman does a fantastic job giving you a sales blueprint with actionable information you can apply. An excellent read whether you are new to sales or have 20 or more years of experience.

> —**Joey Mendoza**, national sales director, HashiCorp; former sales director, VMware; and former senior regional sales manager, Dell

As a product marketing executive, I've worked with salespeople in medium and large IT organizations, as well as startups. Rana's *Sales Essentials* takes you into sellers' minds and provides insights into what effective selling looks like. It's divided into three consumable and easy-to-follow sections, with straightforward advice from a real expert. I recommend this book to sellers, product marketers, and those who work with sales teams.

> —**Arun Lal**, vice president of product marketing, Productiv; former product marketing manager, VMware and Microsoft; and former founder and CMO, Contiq

Rana's book brings all the selling components to life with her straight-from-the-trenches guidance and real-world examples. Her innovative way of explaining what, why, and how to sell makes this book a masterpiece and an essential asset for every seller who is looking to take their performance to the next level.

—**Joanne Moretti**, chief revenue officer, Fictiv

As a sales professor and former sales executive with more than 30 years of experience, I recommend *Sales Essentials* for anyone in the industry—whether you've been selling for years or are just getting started. I will add it as a must-read for my graduate and undergraduate students. It's an end-to-end guide that provides you with everything you need to be successful throughout the sales process, written by someone who not only teaches salespeople how to sell but is also a seller herself. This book is a must-have.

—**Nicolo Alaimo**, professor, Florida International University

SALES
ESSENTIALS

SALES
ESSENTIALS

**THE TOOLS YOU NEED AT EVERY
STAGE TO CLOSE MORE DEALS
AND CRUSH YOUR QUOTA**

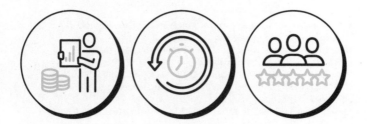

RANA SALMAN, MBA, PhD

Mc
Graw
Hill

NEW YORK   CHICAGO   SAN FRANCISCO   ATHENS   LONDON
MADRID   MEXICO CITY   MILAN   NEW DELHI
SINGAPORE   SYDNEY   TORONTO

1 2 3 4 5 6 7 8 9   LCR   28 27 26 25 24 23

ISBN 978-1-265-22444-8
MHID   1-265-22444-7

e-ISBN 978-1-265-22549-0
e-MHID   1-265-22549-4

Design by Mauna Eichner and Lee Fukui

Library of Congress Cataloging-in-Publication Data

Names: Salman, Rana, author.
Title: Sales essentials : the tools you need at every stage to close more
  deals and crush your quota / Rana Salman.
Description: 1 Edition. | New York : McGraw Hill, [2023] | Includes
  bibliographical references and index.
Identifiers: LCCN 2022059920 (print) | LCCN 2022059921 (ebook) | ISBN
  9781265224448 (hardback) | ISBN 9781265225490 (ebook)
Subjects: LCSH: Selling. | Marketing.
Classification: LCC HF5438.25 .S2543 2023 (print) | LCC HF5438.25 (ebook)
  | DDC 381/.106--dc23/eng/20221215
LC record available at https://lccn.loc.gov/2022059920
LC ebook record available at https://lccn.loc.gov/2022059921

McGraw Hill books are available at special quantity discounts to use as premiums and sales promotions or for use in corporate training programs. To contact a representative, please visit the Contact Us pages at www.mhprofessional.com.

McGraw Hill is committed to making our products accessible to all learners. To learn more about the available support and accommodations we offer, please contact us at accessibility@mheducation.com. We also participate in the Access Text Network (www.accesstext.org), and ATN members may submit requests through ATN.

*To my husband, **Ghassan**, for being my rock and confidant. You have been with me through it all, and I couldn't have gone this far without your support. You love me unconditionally and accept me for who I am. And when I have doubts in myself, you're the first one to gently knock some sense into me.*

*To my two boys, **Samer** and **Zane**, for celebrating every deal I've won and believing in me whenever I hit a speed bump. I still remember when I broke my foot, and you chipped in with your grade-school allowance to help your dad surprise me with a new laptop so I could continue following my passion while I recovered.*

*To my siblings—**Nelma**, **Hiba**, and **Khalil**—for creating a space to dream. You are my best friends for life. We've come a long way, but through it all, we've never lost sight of what's important.*

*And to my parents, **Joumana** and **Abdallah**, who consistently made sacrifices to give us a better life. Dad, you taught me the true meaning of grit, and Mom, you showed me that kindness is a strength. Thank you for cheering us on, keeping us humble, and giving us the opportunity to chase the American dream.*

Contents

PART I

THE ESSENTIALS

PART II

THE ESSENTIALS APPLIED

PART III

BEYOND THE ESSENTIALS

Acknowledgments

I'd like to thank all the teachers I've had throughout my life. I'm eternally grateful that you didn't give up on this immigrant girl and always found time to explain things to me. You saw the spark in my eyes and ignited it. Through you, I fell in love with learning and asking questions. That has served me well in sales!

I want to send special thanks to my customers who believed in me and trusted me. I have immense appreciation for each of you and for your partnership. You challenged my thinking, pushed me at times, collaborated with me to create impactful sales enablement programs, and shared many laughs along the way.

I also can't miss the opportunity to express appreciation to the prospects who listened to my sales pitches over the years—and then either ignored me or told me no. While those experiences may have been painful for both of us, I learned so much from each encounter. Your feedback (in words or in silence) made me stronger and allowed me to grow into the salesperson and consultant I am today.

The other important fuel for my professional development has come in the form of rich discussions with sales, marketing, and enablement colleagues with whom I've been fortunate to cross paths at a variety of venues. I'm extremely thankful for those conversations.

Last but not least, thank you to my editor, Susan Priddy, and the McGraw Hill publishing team led by Cheryl Segura for your guidance, feedback, and insights. You helped me take this book to the next level.

Introduction

There's no other way to say it: I'm absolutely passionate about sales and can't imagine doing anything else for a living. I have extensive experience in the industry and still sell every day. Plus, I have the privilege of developing training programs for sales representatives around the world. Sales is in my blood.

There's just something exciting about figuring out how the products or services I'm selling can solve someone's problems, convincing them of that, and helping them achieve their goals. It's like showing up with the missing puzzle piece that my customers have been searching for. It creates an unmatchable buzz, and I want to share that with you.

WHAT YOU'LL GET FROM THIS BOOK

In the pages ahead, you'll learn about the art and science of sales: the psychology that drives it, the strategies needed for success, the potential challenges involved, and the techniques you can use to overcome those obstacles. It's a start-to-finish look at one of the most fascinating careers in the business world today.

Whether you've been in sales for years or are just beginning your career, this book will guide you in developing the specific skills necessary to succeed in sales at the highest level. Chapter by chapter, you'll discover information that will help you accelerate your sales career and reach your full potential. Like the subtitle says, you'll find out how to close more deals and crush your quota!

I know from experience that being in sales is an extraordinary way to earn a living. It's a career that is somehow thrilling, challenging, rewarding, frustrating, and often lucrative—all at the same time. There's really nothing else quite like it. But when you do it well, you can create the foundation for a lifetime of professional success.

THE BENEFITS YOU'LL GAIN

If you're like me, you want to cut to the chase. Time is money! You just want direct, practical ways to get better at your job, take care of your customers, make money, and meet your quota. "Bottom line it for me!" Fast and straight to the point.

I get it.

I want to honor your busy schedule, so this book is both hard-hitting *and* easy to read. I rolled together specific strategies, personal stories, and solid research into a compelling narrative that can make a measurable difference in your career. It's a highly efficient collection of best practices, all in one spot—and it's exactly what I would want if I were in your position.

I hope the following benefits will be obvious as you read.

Opportunities to Launch and Improve Your Career

If you're committed to enhancing your capabilities, there are always ways to up your game. I want to provide you with guidance to navigate your deals from the beginning to the end—and beyond. And I want to give you the tools you need to be successful.

In this book, I'll tell you straight up what to do and, perhaps more importantly, what *not* to do. You'll get novel insights about the opportunities and pitfalls you'll encounter along the way. And I'll share some of the lessons I've learned throughout my career, including landing multimillion-dollar accounts with midsize to large global organizations, designing enablement solutions to help improve sales performance, and engaging with top reps worldwide.

For some of you, adopting these strategies may change everything you always thought you knew about sales. For others, you may pick up nuggets of wisdom that allow you to make incremental improvements that completely transform your potential.

Either way, your sales career will get a boost if you actively apply the techniques and best practices in this book.

Opportunities to Make Money

In many cases, organizations have competitive compensation structures and strong product portfolios. If they also have the right engagement models, systems, and culture, the salespeople working for those companies can basically write their own tickets. The only limits on their salaries are the number of hours in a day and their capacity for hard work.

Think about knowing some of the most critical strategies and tactics for a job with almost unlimited income potential. This book gives you that information.

Opportunities for Job Security

The ability to sell—and do it well—is a skill that translates across all industries, all geographic boundaries, and all business sizes and types.

If you move to another city or decide to work in a different industry, sales jobs are almost always available.

Companies fail if they can't sell their products or services. If you can be the person to help them do that successfully, you'll become an influential and pivotal part of thriving organizations—wherever you go. If you can sell, you have a level of job security that doesn't come with many other careers.

The following pages are your gateway to that financial safety net.

Opportunities to Increase Your Influence

In some respects, every person on the planet is in sales—regardless of their backgrounds or the titles on their business cards. We have to sell ourselves and our résumés to gain employment. We have to sell our ideas to our managers to compete for budget dollars or the chance to lead the best projects. We have to sell our colleagues on concepts for initiatives. And hey, we might have to sell our significant others on going to Hawaii for vacation or purchasing a vintage sports car.

Reading this book is a smart way to become more influential in many areas of your life!

Opportunities to Differentiate Yourself

The reality is most salespeople have a strong competitive streak. We love to win. It's probably in our DNA. And that's why you're going to love this book. It will give you the shortcuts you need to get noticed and get ahead.

By taking a fresh and sometimes unexpected look at your career in sales, you'll have a new perspective from which to pursue success. You'll also gain skills that can add value to your life in multiple ways.

That means generating efficiencies that optimize your time, at work and at home. Establishing yourself as a leader in your company. Differentiating yourself to land major deals that give you the financial flexibility to create the life you want.

All of that is possible if you apply the best practices discussed in the chapters ahead.

HOW THIS BOOK IS ORGANIZED

This book is conveniently divided into three parts that will guide you through your deals in a practical, accessible way.

In Part I, "The Essentials," you'll explore the foundation for the sales experience, take a closer look at the challenges involved, and discover the characteristics needed to excel in this career choice.

Moving into Part II, "The Essentials Applied," you'll complete a preliminary benchmark assessment to help you target opportunities for growth. Then you'll take a chronological journey into sales with granular descriptions of steps before, during, and after the sale. Each of those sections concludes with a real-world scenario that allows you to translate your knowledge about sales into actual decision-making and strategic implementation.

In Part III, "Beyond the Essentials," you'll find valuable information about the psychological aspects of sales—dealing with rejection and self-doubt. More importantly, you'll learn about specific tactics to help protect your mental health.

As a bonus, I've provided a Sales Essentials Toolkit that includes checklists and templates you can populate to accelerate your mastery of the sales process.

I hope you'll find this book to be comprehensive and compelling. Are you ready to get started?

SALES
ESSENTIALS

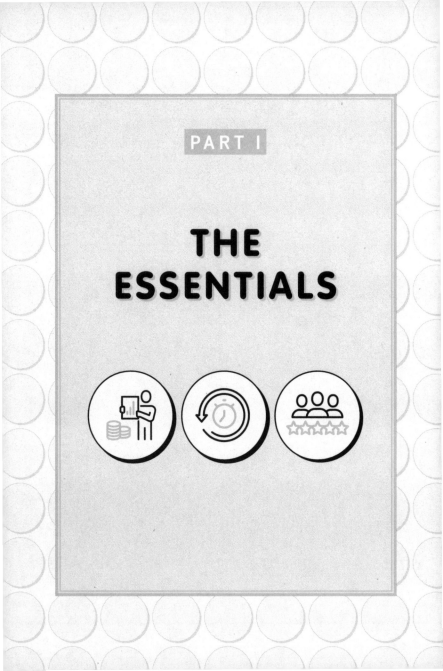

PART I

THE ESSENTIALS

The Heart of Sales

When talking about sales today, statistics often dominate the conversation: quotas, number of leads in the pipeline, conversion rates, monthly recurring revenue, and opportunity-to-win ratios, just to name a few.

All those things are critical, without a doubt. But they don't even come close to the real foundation for the timeless skill of selling. I know about this from personal experience.

Decades ago, I went on my first sales call. I was nine years old.

We lived in Lebanon at the time, and the country was in the midst of a civil war. Jobs were scarce, but my dad sold insurance solutions door-to-door. Somehow my parents always managed to find work that allowed them to take care of our family.

I can't remember how I convinced my dad to take me with him to a sales meeting that particular day. But selfishly, I do remember I wanted to go because the potential customer lived in a chalet at the beach. Going to the meeting was just an excuse to spend a few hours next to the sea.

As we drove in the old red Datsun, I sat quietly listening to him recite some of his prepared statements for the appointment. My dad went through his opening comments, agenda, and product descriptions. Watching him, I learned that sales really required discipline. What happened before the call was crucial, and winging it was not an option. In his case, practice was literally the key to survival.

He paused and said a little prayer as we made it closer to the beach house. There was no chitchatting between us. He was focused, and we both knew it was "showtime." We pulled up to the chalet and climbed out of the car. Dressed in his nicest suit, he grasped his black suitcase and held my hand tightly in the other.

I could tell my dad was nervous. But the minute he was in front of his prospects, he transformed. He stood up straight, shoulders back, and flashed a warm smile. He confidently greeted the husband and wife by their names and introduced me to them. They chatted briefly about their children and current events.

While I don't recall many details of the meeting, what I learned that day has somehow stuck with me for decades. I could tell that my father genuinely liked these people. He cared about them, and he wanted to help them find what they needed to make their lives better.

My impatient, nine-year-old self assumed this would be a quick transaction. I guess I expected him to pop open his briefcase and offer them Option A or Option B. They'd pick one, and I'd soon be dipping my toes in the ocean.

That's not how it happened.

Instead, my dad took time to listen and ask targeted questions. He gently nodded while the husband and wife answered. He was very specific, and he took notes. Knowing my dad, I'm sure his brain was spinning with ideas as he looked back at his notes to come up with a customized solution.

This wasn't the last time I saw my dad engaging with his customers. As I got older, I asked why he didn't just jump into describing his offerings for the prospects instead of taking time to gather so much information. Wouldn't that be faster and more efficient? His answer was not what I expected.

He explained that these people weren't just potential customers; they were human beings with lives and families and dreams, as well as doubts and fears. He wasn't just trying to sell them insurance; he wanted to get to know them. He sincerely wanted to help them get the security and peace of mind they needed to protect the people they loved in the event of an emergency.

That didn't sound like a sales call to me. It was something else, although I couldn't put my finger on it at the time. Eventually, with a few years and some life experiences under my belt, it made perfect sense.

What my dad demonstrated for me that day at the beach and in many other customer interactions was the human connection that's at the heart of every sale. This book will help you discover that for yourself—and so much more.

CHANGING YOUR MINDSET

Even though we all have goals to meet, the quickest way to fail is to take the human element out of the sales equation. Our prospects shouldn't represent dollar signs or quota fillers. Sure, it's an easy error to make. When we're facing the chaos of uncertain situations, there's something tangible (and even comforting) about slicing and dicing the data. Analyzing the numbers is in our comfort zone.

But even though the quantitative side is critical, we can't lose sight of the big picture—behind every data point is a story. Each bit of data represents a customer trying to solve a problem or drive an initiative.

By accepting and embracing that concept, you approach the sales process with a more productive mindset. In other words, your objective shifts from an internal focus on "winning the deal" to an external focus on "helping the customer be successful." You are less driven by your own goals in favor of helping customers meet theirs. And although this might sound like counterintuitive thinking, that attitude can catapult you into top-tier salesperson status.

Here's my challenge to you. As you review the data related to a possible sale, stop to look at the human part of the equation and take an outside-in perspective. You'll quickly find that this shift prompts you to *expand* the questions you ask and the strategy you follow.

For instance, you might initially hope to find answers to questions like these:

- What's the budget?

- How can I make sure I'm not leaving money on the table?

- What's the timeline?

- How soon can I get an appointment with the decision maker?

- How much effort will I have to invest to close the deal?

- How do I avoid red tape in the approval process?

- Will this sale hit the books in time to count toward my quarterly goal?

If you adjust your mindset to incorporate the human component of the sale, you'll dig deeper and answer some additional questions:

- Who is the customer, professionally and personally?

- What role do they play in the organization?

- What initiatives are they personally working on?

- How can I partner with them to help reach their goals?

- What problems do they need to solve?

- How can I help them be successful—now and in the future?

The insights you gain from those human-focused questions will give you a real edge in the sales process. Here's an example of what that looks like.

Imagine you are selling a portfolio of technology products and have identified a prime prospect. You've done online research to learn more about the company and the potential buyer, familiarizing yourself with the person behind the title.

As you conduct the discovery meeting, you keep the conversation focused on the prospect and her world, avoiding the urge to jump right into your product features and benefits. You already know from your research that the potential buyer is new to her leadership role, and she emphasizes several times this is a highly visible initiative with top executive scrutiny. You recognize the business problem she's trying to solve, the pressure she's under to deliver results, and her desire to showcase innovative thinking to the leadership team.

Keeping that human factor in mind, you design a customized solution that not only solves the problem identified but also positions her as an innovator with strategic vision. Your proposal and presentation demonstrate you are a partner committed to helping her reach corporate objectives *and* personal career goals. She recognizes both sides of the value and champions your proposal with all key decision makers. The final contract is larger than you originally anticipated.

Finding that human angle is definitely one of your competitive advantages as a salesperson.

UNDERSTANDING THE MOTIVES

Another benefit of looking at sales through a human lens is the way it can change your perspective. If my goal is to help my customers be successful, I automatically consider us to be on the same side rather than adversaries. It gives me more empathy. That's important when the typical sales roadblocks start to build frustration.

As part of my consulting practice, I coached a salesperson who found himself in that position. His deal was stuck because of questions from the customer's finance department, and he was visibly annoyed. "These people have no idea what my products can do," he said. "They are just trying to cut costs. They don't get it." He told me several times that he just needed 10 minutes to convince them that rejecting his proposal would be a huge mistake.

I challenged him to step back from the frustration and look at the situation in a different way: from the customer's point of view. After he gave that direction some thought, he took my advice.

He started by researching the names of the people in the customer's finance department. He checked them out on LinkedIn, learning more about them and their roles. By humanizing these professionals, he was able to unpack their motives and see things from their perspective.

They were getting intense pressure from investors and shareholders after two quarters of lower-than-expected financial performance. Signing off on his proposal seemed like it involved taking on a significant amount of risk.

Once he understood their perception of this transaction, he was able to reframe his attitude and his approach in working with them. He changed his thinking from *How can I convince them they are wrong?* to *How can I help them make the best possible decision, given their unique challenges?*

He took the time to schedule an appointment with the CFO and his direct reports, positioning himself as a partner rather than a salesperson. He shared his return on investment (ROI) calculations and described the bottom-line benefits his products could generate. He spoke their language and, most importantly, he demonstrated he wanted to *help* them rather than *fight* them.

Based on my experience, that collaboration always sets the stage for more positive outcomes. And, in fact, it worked well for this salesperson. His extra effort to understand the challenges his clients were facing was rewarded with a promptly signed contract.

SETTING YOURSELF APART

When you approach sales as opportunities to help people reach their goals or solve their problems, you'll inevitably close more deals. That wisdom applies whether you're selling a $1,000 product or a $10 million enterprise solution. But the advantage doesn't stop there. You'll also stand out from the crowd as someone with insight and integrity who genuinely cares about others. As a tool for sales career longevity, it doesn't get much better than that.

If you want to fuel your long-term success as a salesperson, make a commitment to an attitude of *customer centricity*. Management consulting company Gartner, Inc., defines that as "the focal point of all decisions related to delivering products, services, and experiences to create customer satisfaction, loyalty, and advocacy."[1] In other words, it's about putting the customer at the center of your universe. That choice is never wrong if you're interested in pursuing professional advancement.

While the human angle of sales may be overlooked and undervalued at times, it's one of the most important components in your success. When you clearly display respect and positive intent—in the way you show up, the way you talk, the way you honor an investment of time—prospects and buyers can see your commitment to working with them. They will feel like collaborative partners rather than boxes to be checked. That emotional connection assures them that you are personally dedicated to delivering on your promises.

As you continue reading, you'll find that the human component at the heart of sales is the all-important thread that runs throughout this book and ties everything together.

ESSENTIAL TAKEAWAYS

At the end of each chapter, you'll find Essential Takeaways. These are the most important points you'll need to carry into your professional and personal lives to find lasting success. In this chapter, the Essential Takeaways are:

- Successful salespeople recognize that human connection and relationships are at the heart of every sale.

- The most effective sales strategy is to approach potential deals as opportunities to help people solve their problems or reach their goals.

- Changing your mindset to pursue the human angle of sales can give you a distinct competitive advantage.

- Humanizing your prospects and buyers will help you understand their perspectives and better meet their needs.

- Salespeople can set themselves apart by demonstrating their commitment to be a collaborative partner rather than simply a vendor.

The Challenges of Sales

If someone tells you selling is easy, they probably haven't done it consistently. Especially enterprise-wide, business-to-business (B2B) sales, where the complexity can be astronomical.

The statistics tell the story. In a 2019 Salesforce State of Sales research survey of 2,900 sales professionals worldwide, 57 percent of representatives expected to miss their quotas that year.[1] Another survey from the software-as-a-service (SaaS) firm Xactly found companies are struggling to keep their sales reps, with 58 percent reporting a high voluntary turnover rate.[2] Quitting is common. The pandemic made things worse, prompting many salespeople to look for new jobs with greater flexibility.

Think about what that says. More than half of the current salespeople are likely frustrated with their situations, as are their sales managers. If reps choose to leave (or are asked to leave), they are walking away from their salaries, benefits, and established customers. But the price is also high for their companies. Hiring and training are expensive. According to the Work Institute 2020 Retention Report, the cost of employee turnover adds up to about 30 percent of their salaries.[3]

Despite all the advantages, a career in sales comes with its own set of challenges. Thankfully, there are ways you can mitigate those.

INTERNAL CHALLENGES

Some challenges facing sales reps today stem from issues within the corporate culture. While we won't specifically talk here about the importance of sales leaders in addressing these challenges (a topic for another book!), they are a pivotal part of the equation—just keep that in mind. In the meantime, I'll describe some of the problems within your control and offer a few potential solutions.

Unrealistic Expectations

Let's be honest. In some organizations, salespeople are expected to produce at superhuman levels. Every quarter . . . every year . . . no excuses. The constant pressure is sometimes unsustainable, and I hear about this problem from reps across the globe:

- "When we get close to achieving our quotas, they change them."

- "The goals they set aren't even remotely grounded in the real world."

- "It's like we're being punished if we meet our quotas because they just keep raising them."

You've probably uttered one of those statements yourself, right? I know I have. So what can you do about it?

Solutions

Schedule a meeting to talk with your supervisor and prepare a list of points you'd like to cover. Approach that conversation with the goal of sharing information.

Explain your perspective and ask thoughtful questions. Are there valid reasons behind an overly ambitious quota? How is the company enabling you to reach those goals? Is the compensation fair? While it's unlikely your manager can move the goalpost based on a single request, your input could prompt this person to have conversations with other salespeople and, potentially, reevaluate the expectations.

Once you've planted that seed, you may want to consider an attitude check. Could your frustrations with the system be inadvertently holding you back? Are there ways you can challenge yourself to make progress without getting bogged down in defeat every time you look at those overly ambitious goals?

Finally, hit pause on everything you're doing. If your current approach isn't getting you where you need to be, what could you change? What shifts could you make that disrupt your usual process? Sometimes you've got to shake things up to get a different result. More on that coming up.

Complex Portfolios

Another internal challenge enterprise reps face is the large product portfolios they're expected to remember and understand—on a detailed level. Sometimes I'm blown away by the sheer volume of components, especially when products are continually added to portfolios through aggressive research and development (R&D) or acquisitions. What they're selling becomes a constantly moving target. As things evolve, every business unit (BU) is pushing for their products to be included in as many deals as possible. To do that, these BUs want to stay top of mind with the people in customer-facing roles. In other words, competition for the salesperson's mental bandwidth can sometimes be intense. It's not surprising when I hear comments like this:

- "OK, wait. What is this again?"

- "How does this fit in with the rest of our solution?"

- "Why should I include it? I'm not even getting paid for it!"

On some level, organizations must recognize that portfolios are becoming unwieldy. A 2020 study by global management consulting firm McKinsey & Company found that 40 percent of executives reported postpandemic plans to reduce their product portfolios and reallocate budgets.[4] In fact, one company reduced its portfolio from 800 product variants to 25. That change, along with initiatives to shorten lead times and create a better customer experience, resulted in a 5 percent increase in sales while reducing costs significantly.[5]

The streamlining trend may be on the rise, but the current reality remains. There's still a lot of work to be done to simplify product portfolios today.

Solutions

Start by focusing on what you *can* control. If you've moved to sell for a new organization, how well do you know the primary products? Which ones align with the company's core strategy and meet customers' needs? Which ones are linked to the metrics that measure your performance? If you're not sure which products to focus on first, who can clarify that for you? Make sure to do your part to increase your knowledge level.

Second, keep the emphasis on your customers. Do you have a solid understanding of their needs? If you approach your portfolio from that angle, you can look at your products and services as a buffet of options to help your customers solve their problems and achieve their objectives. That reduces the pressure of trying to find a way to sell everything.

Finally, be proactive about sharing feedback regarding the portfolio with your sales leaders. You have a frontline perspective that makes your opinions extremely valuable. If there's a disconnect between some of the pieces or if the complexity is undermining your ability to sell, executives need to know.

Internal Politics

When selling enterprise deals, you have to work closely with a wide range of people inside your organization. There's no other way around it. And that means navigating the sometimes murky waters of internal politics. It's frustrating and exhausting. But it's also an inevitable part of the game.

You've probably been pursuing a big account with great enthusiasm, only to pick up the phone or receive an email that adds internal friction to your sales process:

- "You really shouldn't have said that in front of the regional VP."

- "You're using a deck with messaging that isn't approved."

- "You're not following the proper protocol."

Sometimes those comments are valid—but sometimes they aren't. Either way, it's important to recognize personal agendas exist and be sensitive to the impact your words and actions have on others within your organization.

Another layer to the internal politics is the general bureaucracies that drag out the sales process—multiple systems, long review and approval chains, unfortunate redundancies, and even lack of clarity on roles and responsibilities. Those factors can undermine the performance of sales reps and even prompt them to walk away from jobs with never-ending red tape.

Solutions

First, accept the reality that internal politics are part of every business landscape. Wishing they didn't exist is wasted energy. You simply need to find a way to manage those nuances so they don't impact your deals and customers.

Next, make sure you fully understand which people or departments internally should be involved in your sale. What roles and responsibilities are included? Ask questions about the level of interaction and chain of command. Communicate openly with the appropriate people to ensure no one feels left out of the process. As you move through deals, share insights with your boss about how the integration of efforts is working and highlight any stumbling blocks.

Be deliberate about trying to see the perspectives of the other people involved and demonstrating empathy. By putting ourselves in their shoes, we can better understand the challenges and obstacles they face. Everyone has a job to do, and it always helps to give people the benefit of the doubt.

Finally, don't avoid addressing any conflicts. Without a discussion, they'll only snowball and end up bigger than they really are.

Too Many Tools (or Not Enough)

I'm a big fan of using technology to improve sales efficiencies and elevate the customer experience. If companies aren't supplying the tools required, salespeople may be facing an uphill battle.

On the other hand, I've also seen technology overload create a nightmare for reps. It is easy to feel overwhelmed if there are too many different tools and systems (especially those that aren't integrated) or not enough training on how to use them.

The 2017 State of Sales report from InsideSales found that, on average, companies have 5.8 sales tools to support their reps' efforts.[6] And it's not slowing down. LinkedIn's State of Sales Report 2021 indicated that "77% of sales professionals say their [organization] plans to invest more in sales intelligence tools."[7]

Solutions

Is your organization providing the appropriate technology tools to be efficient in your job? Be aware of what's currently available and make sure to fully leverage those assets.

If you believe your ability to sell is being hindered by a lack of tools, talk with your boss and describe the specific challenges you're facing. Explain what type of tools could help you land more deals and request that the appropriate internal team investigate the options. And if you have recommendations, be sure to share them.

If you have too many tools at your disposal, pinpoint the benefits of each one. Are there any redundancies or conflicts? If you determine a particular tool isn't helping you achieve your objectives and, worse yet, wasting your time, you may have some solid arguments for not using it. Just be sure to consider what benefits you might lose if you decide to let one go.

Too Much Training (or Not Enough)

This category echoes the arguments in the previous section about the overabundance or lack of technology tools. There's a fine line between having too much and too little sales training.

If you're required to attend endless training sessions, that seriously cuts into your time to sell. But if you aren't offered anything at all, you may feel like you are floundering when it comes to your knowledge of the solution portfolio—how to sell it, how to identify the right target audience, and how you are different than the competition.

Solutions

Be open with your supervisor and trusted sales enablement colleagues about whether the level of training offered is sufficient. Do you feel like something's missing? Or has it started to seem like busywork? Have candid discussions with your sales and enablement leaders about where you need development help to improve your performance.

If your organization cannot provide any additional training, seek out your own options to help fill those gaps. You'll find plenty of opportunities to uplevel your skills—from books and workshops to webinars and online courses. Taking control of your own professional development makes a bold statement about your career priorities.

EXTERNAL CHALLENGES

While we have some control over the internal sales environment, the external components present more challenges—or at least demand more flexibility.

External Challenges

Shifting sales approach

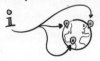

The changing needs of enterprise customers

The Shifting Sales Approach

The traditional picture in our heads of the perfect sales meeting might look something like this: sitting at a table face-to-face with a prospect, enjoying some coffee, and talking about ways to solve the company's problems. In many ways, the global business environment and Covid-19 have taken a hammer to that image.

Prospects may be located on the other side of the world. Traveling across the globe involves a significant investment of time and money, not to mention the hassles of potential travel delays and flight cancellations. For those and other reasons, virtual meetings have become an acceptable alternative in the world of sales during the past few years.

But what about the future? What's ahead for B2B sales?

The answer appears to be a hybrid solution—a combination of some in-person meetings supported by virtual contacts. After surveying more than 2,500 sales organizations, management consultants McKinsey & Company found that a hybrid approach "is expected to be the most dominant sales strategy by 2024."[8] The study results emphasized the need for sellers to offer "in-person, remote, and digital self-serve interactions in equal measures if they want to meet the buyers' expectations."[9]

Customer preferences are definitely driving this shift. In another study with 3,626 B2B decision makers, McKinsey's research showed that 70–80 percent of decision makers "prefer remote human interactions or digital self-service."[10] In addition, 70 percent of customers claim "they are open to making new, fully self-serve or remote purchases for more than $50,000."[11] Perhaps even more surprising, 27 percent of those surveyed said they would spend more than $500,000 on a self-serve or remote transaction.[12]

The point is, our comfort level with the virtual world has grown by leaps and bounds.

That's great news for salespeople, as confirmed by the McKinsey study. The research indicated that "remote sales reps can reach four times as many accounts in the same amount of time and generate up to 50 percent more revenue."[13] Efficiency, off the charts!

I do want to add a word of caution though. Efficiency has its limits, which is why the hybrid approach to sales brings in the best of both worlds.

Never underestimate the impact of in-person meetings. There's science behind the power of physical presence. It builds connection and trust in ways that aren't possible through virtual contact or an email. Yes, in-person meetings require more time and effort, but they are worth it. By combining the more tangible connection of face-to-face meetings with the efficiency of virtual contact, you can overcome some obvious hurdles and create a streamlined process that generates greater results.

As you embrace the concept of hybrid selling, be sure to adapt to your customers' needs. Don't assume a 50/50 split between in-person and remote meetings will be appropriate for every account. Some customers prefer more face-to-face contact, and you'll want to honor that. When you're trying to qualify an opportunity and land a new deal, an in-person conversation may be the most effective option.

Be flexible and find the balance between personal connection and efficiency that maximizes your sales.

The Changing Needs of Enterprise Customers

The organizations we serve with our sales solutions are undergoing continuous and often rapid evolution. Compare enterprise customers today with those of 30 years ago. The differences can be defined by the impact of new laws and regulations, advanced technology, the growth and complexity of data, the globalization of business, and a more distributed workforce. Toss in factors like pandemics and the political climate, and you can see that customers are facing challenges now they couldn't even have imagined years ago.

Their needs have changed dramatically, and that affects those of us in sales. Let's look at the impact of those changes in several examples.

First, potential customers historically expected sellers to provide all the information needed about potential solutions. Today, the internet gives them a wealth of data at their fingertips, allowing them to do extensive research before they ever have a conversation with us. Some prospects even wonder if they really need to talk with us at all.

Our challenge as salespeople is to show them that we can add extraordinary guidance, innovative thinking, and value when it comes to complex enterprise solutions. That doesn't involve making them feel even more overwhelmed by loading them down with additional reams of data. They look to us to help make sense of the information and share our insights on the meaning.[14]

Next, large companies are often geographically dispersed with organization charts that are sometimes convoluted. The days of having a single customer contact are gone. If salespeople haven't already adjusted to that fact, they need to. In most cases, there are several decision makers around the globe involved in approving our enterprise solutions. It's our job in this environment to use the tools at our disposal to connect with each of those individuals as part of securing our deals.

This is challenging. Each of those people has his or her own objectives, challenges, and concerns. Salespeople need to work to understand those differentiations and customize conversations. By showing decision makers how our products and services add value to meet their unique needs, we are layering in greater potential for success in landing enterprise deals.

Internally and externally, sales reps will always have obstacles to overcome. The upside? There are more things within our control than we might first think. Being proactive about managing challenges while being flexible to meet customers' needs allows us to demonstrate our commitment to their accounts. Even better, that's a great way to position ourselves as their partners.

ESSENTIAL TAKEAWAYS

- Despite the many benefits, a career in sales comes with a number of internal and external challenges.

- Salespeople may have to navigate unrealistic expectations, complex portfolios, internal politics, and inadequate levels of tools and training.

- The sales environment is shifting to a hybrid model of virtual and in-person selling that expands market opportunities but also creates logistical challenges.

- Enterprise customers have access to vast amounts of information, so they expect salespeople to help them make sense of it all and add value.

- Being flexible and proactive about meeting these challenges is the key for salespeople to succeed.

Characteristics of Successful Salespeople

I've spent time around thousands of highly respected salespeople throughout my career and have the honor of training many more through my consulting business today. While they all have distinct personalities, I've noticed some traits that seem to be consistent across the other variations. Great sellers generally tend to be confident, persistent, collaborative, and resilient. With that said, research also indicates an expanding set of qualities needed for sales success in today's fast-moving, highly competitive business environment.

Results from a 2022 study published in *Harvard Business Review* highlighted the emerging characteristics companies look for in salespeople.[1] The study reviewed more than 20,000 job postings from 2019 to 2022 and identified that modern sellers need the ability to:

- Anticipate customers' needs

- Collaborate effectively inside and outside the organization

- Efficiently utilize digital and virtual channels

- Evaluate and use complex data analytics

- Adapt quickly to change

This research confirms the trend to hire salespeople with attributes that elevate their influence in customer relationships. As an example, the article describes the hiring process for sales account executives (AEs) at Microsoft. Experience and motivation are now just baseline requirements. Instead, Microsoft searches for those who "sell their cloud services to digital native startup customers to 'understand how startup businesses grow and mature their commercial models' so AEs can get an agenda-setting seat at the buyer's table."[2]

That concept—having a seat at the buyer's table—captures the difference between successful salespeople today versus 20 years ago. It's all about having characteristics and skills that move you from vendor to a trusted consultant and partner. Admittedly, that raises the bar for salespeople to adopt critical leadership skills that ensure they're worthy of that seat at the table.

Particularly in the arena of complex enterprise sales, the idea of merging traditional sales skills with leadership competencies is extremely important. Of course, there are thousands of resources available to help improve your leadership skills. However, one umbrella characteristic is pivotal in transforming garden-variety salespeople into world-class sales partners: *self-awareness*. It's a buzzword often mentioned but frequently glossed over. "Sure, self-awareness must be important because everybody talks about it. But it's also a little vague. I mean, of course, I'm aware of myself. Right . . . ?"

Here's the problem. According to research reported in *Harvard Business Review* by executive development firm Eurich Group,

95 percent of people claim to be self-aware when, in fact, only 10 to 15 percent genuinely display that quality.[3] That's quite a gap in perception, and it's a discrepancy that can seriously undermine success.

A top example of how much most people lack self-awareness is found when they are asked how well they listen to others. Inevitably, they say something like: "Oh yes, I'm a great listener." But if their bosses, colleagues, or partners are asked, it would probably be a different answer.

What does this reveal? Most of us tend to overestimate our abilities. We might think we're self-aware, but reality may not match up.

SELF-AWARENESS

Let's take a closer look at *self-awareness*—what it is, why it matters in sales, and how to strengthen it for a distinct career advantage.

The Definition

In its simplest form, people with strong self-awareness understand who they really are internally and know what drives them. They have an accurate view of their own personalities, strengths, weaknesses, emotions, and responses.[4]

They also have a keen awareness of external factors. They recognize how they're being perceived by people around them and can accurately judge how their words and actions impact others.[5]

This combo platter of internal and external awareness makes them truly self-aware and socially savvy. Plus, it fuels an appealing sense of charisma that walks the tightrope between confidence and humility. In sales, that's a winning combination!

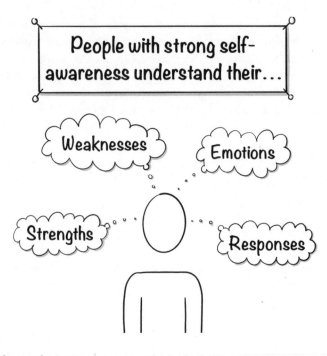

The Value

If you have any doubts about whether self-awareness is really important, it is. And if I can't convince you, let the research do it.

Studies show that people with high levels of self-awareness are happier, more confident, and make better decisions.[6] They are also more likely to be strong leaders and better salespeople with greater potential for promotions.[7]

In case you're wondering, organizations reap the benefits, too. Consulting firm Korn Ferry International analyzed nearly 7,000 self-assessments from employees at 486 publicly traded companies while monitoring the rate of return for those organizations' stocks over a 30-month period. Companies with professionals who rated higher on self-awareness consistently outperformed those with employees who gave themselves lower scores. In fact, according to the study, employees working for organizations with poor financial performance were "79 percent more likely to have low overall self-awareness than those at firms with a robust rate of return."[8]

The Strategies

According to experts, self-awareness is a skill everyone can work to acquire and to develop through practice.[9] That's great news for any salesperson. If you grow those skills by applying the targeted strategies that follow, you will improve your capacity for selling at the highest level.

Prioritize Self-Discovery

There are many ways to discover more about yourself, including taking a standardized personality test, keeping a journal to track your thoughts and emotions, practicing mindfulness/meditation, and reading books about self-awareness. It's also important to think deeply about how the elements of who you are either propel you to action or prevent you from moving forward. For example, what strengths and weaknesses are you working with? What personal characteristics set you apart—or tend to cause you problems? To capitalize on what makes you exceptional or fix what's holding you back, you must be self-aware.

Self-awareness also gives real clarity about our values, beliefs, and passions. In sales, the pressure to close deals and win accounts may make it harder to do the right things. But when we know exactly who we are and what we stand for, we also know where to draw the line. Some things are just nonnegotiable. Having that awareness is an essential part of selling with integrity.

Gather Feedback

Since the perceptions of our own self-awareness are often inaccurate, it's important to get some outside opinions. As a first step, ask several people you trust for their constructive feedback about your impact on others.

For more comprehensive and anonymous input, you could also use a 360° assessment. I was in my late thirties the first time I participated in one of these formal evaluations, and it was an eye-opening experience. Part surprise, part cringe.

I viewed myself as an efficient seller and celebrated my "get-it-done" attitude. I firmly believed people around me saw those qualities as positive. After all, I was landing deals and bringing in revenue.

So, I was blindsided to discover that my intensity and heightened sense of urgency stressed and overwhelmed those around me. It was definitely not what I expected to hear and proved I had work to do. Chances are, you'll uncover something similar that needs your attention when you ask for feedback—and that's OK!

As a salesperson, the feedback you collect may help you answer some important questions:

- Do you come across as having a positive or negative attitude?

- Do you engage in dialogue with others, or does it feel more like an interrogation?

- Do you listen carefully or repeatedly interrupt?

- Do you speak clearly and concisely? Or do you ramble?

- Are you seen as a team player?

- Do you provide the right amount of information or sabotage your own deals by overtalking and overselling?

Pinpoint Areas for Development

Once you identify any gaps in your skills, work on addressing them to improve your performance.

For example, I know something important about myself—I'm impatient. Always have been. Probably always will be. But being aware of that gives me a chance to self-regulate this weakness. In fact, I've come to recognize the physical manifestations of that feeling—which, for me, includes touching my neck, rubbing my temples, or finishing other people's sentences. Now, when I notice those signs of impatience that's an important heads-up to closely monitor my emotions and reactions. Am I inadvertently frowning? Are my conversations getting snippy? Am I unconsciously shaking my leg under the desk?

I've accepted this part of myself by now and realize I'm still going to feel impatient on the inside sometimes. But self-awareness allows me to recognize that sensation bubbling up so I can adjust my behavior. Without those changes, I would inadvertently shut down two-way discussions that could give me valuable access to others' perspectives.

Learn to Manage the Way You're Perceived

I'm always surprised when people in a professional setting follow up some type of questionable comment or behavior with a statement like this: "I'm just being me. Why can't you accept me the way I am?" They've bought into the whole what-you-see-is-what-you-get concept. Somehow they've convinced themselves that we'll excuse almost anything under the guise of being "authentic."

As you might guess, that's not always a positive approach.

Especially in sales, we can't afford to communicate with others and *not* pay attention to the impact we're having—positive or negative. The perceptions of the people around us matter—to our relationships and our success. We need self-awareness to recognize how others perceive us and quickly address any gaps we identify.

Strategies to Expand Your Self-Awareness

Prioritize self-discovery

Gather feedback

Pinpoint areas for development

Learn to manage the way you're perceived

It's not always easy to admit our limitations. In fact, it can be a very humbling experience to find out we're not doing something as well as we thought. But those realizations also give us something very important: control over the situation. Once we're aware and take action to make improvements, we become better sellers and better partners to customers and colleagues.

These strategies to improve self-awareness are just the beginning. Throughout this book, you'll discover additional tips and best practices to help you adopt the attributes found in world-class sellers.

• • •

Congratulations on making your way through the essentials of sales. You've learned about the importance of the human connection in the sales process, the potential obstacles you may encounter, and the characteristics most critical for your success.

Next, you'll have a chance to take a benchmark self-assessment that will help you pinpoint your current level of self-awareness and sales mastery compared with best practices. Armed with your results, you'll be ready to dive into some strategies that help you accelerate your career success and apply the essentials before, during, and after every sale.

ESSENTIAL TAKEAWAYS

- Successful salespeople tend to have some common attributes, such as confidence, persistence, resilience, and a collaborative spirit.

- Salespeople today can elevate their impact with buyers by incorporating leadership skills that position them as partners and trusted consultants.

- Many characteristics that contribute to sales success fall into the category of self-awareness.

- People who are self-aware have an accurate view of their strengths, weaknesses, emotions, and responses, and recognize how they're being perceived by those around them.

- To improve self-awareness, salespeople should prioritize self-discovery, gather feedback, pinpoint areas for development, and actively manage the way they're perceived by others.

PART II

THE ESSENTIALS APPLIED

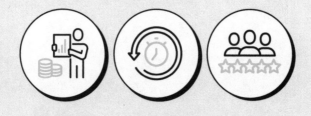

Sales Self-Assessment

Now that you understand the essentials, you're ready to *apply* the essentials. To get started, complete the benchmark below. Your answers will help highlight the areas you can target in Part II to make the most dramatic improvement in your sales techniques. No one else needs to see this, so feel free to be brutally honest.

Directions: Please read each statement and use the following scale to indicate how strongly you agree with it. Then add up the rating column for a total score at the bottom.

1 = Never
2 = Rarely
3 = Sometimes
4 = Usually
5 = Always

Rating	
	I use social media to engage with my prospects and existing customers.
	I schedule time for prospecting every week.
	I use research to learn about the needs of my prospects and the positioning of their organizations.
	I prepare for discovery meetings by searching for similarities and common interests with my prospects that could support my rapport-building efforts.
	I recognize the impact of first impressions on my ability to sell.

	I structure my sales calls to include making introductions, getting agreement on the agenda, and building rapport.
	I use my discovery meetings to engage in business-level conversations that focus on my buyers' world.
	I pay attention to my prospects' body language and facial expressions during discovery meetings and adjust my presentations accordingly.
	I validate my research during discovery meetings and qualify opportunities by asking targeted, relevant questions.
	I discuss the next steps in detail with prospects before the conclusion of my discovery meetings.
	I follow up with my prospects within 24 hours after discovery meetings to demonstrate my responsiveness and summarize our discussions.
	I align my solutions with prospects' needs and highlight the benefits most important to them.
	I share insights with my prospects and find ways to add value for them before, during, and after my discovery meetings.
	I provide real-world evidence of success that is relevant to my buyers during sales calls.
	I provide complete information to any teammates involved in my deals to help them understand the buyers' needs and expectations.

	I work to understand my prospects' internal decision-making processes once I qualify opportunities.
	I understand the roles and needs of the different stakeholders within my prospects' organizations.
	I customize my demo talks to align with the needs of my prospects.
	I look for opportunities to upsell and cross-sell within my existing accounts.
	I ask for referrals as part of my sales process.
	Maximum Score: 100

Add up your total score to determine your percentage of the 100 possible points. This score is only the "starting line"—a way to help measure your progress as you learn more about sales applications in this Part, "The Essentials Applied." Once you've had a chance to practice new sales strategies, you can repeat this assessment to track your growth.

Right now, this benchmark assessment can also help you gain some valuable insights into your specific sales skill levels. Any statements that you ranked as a 4 or 5 may represent your strengths. Statements that you ranked as a 1, 2, or 3 provide you with opportunities for improvement.

Circle or highlight the three to five statements with the lowest scores. As you work through Part II and begin to practice some of your sales skills in real time, pay close attention to those specific areas. If you focus on accelerating those particular skills, you'll likely see the biggest change in your sales performance and results.

CHAPTER
4

Know Your Product

Now that we understand the essentials of selling, including the challenges faced in sales and the characteristics of successful salespeople, it's time to move to applying the essentials. In this part of the book, you'll explore the anatomy of selling and get an up-close view of each step involved before, during, and after the sale.

Most people recognize the key to selling value in enterprise deals is to focus on the customers and their businesses—*not* to lead with the solution. However, before we can sell value, we need to know the fundamentals of our product: What is it? How does it work? Who needs it? And how does it compare with other available solutions?

To close deals, we have to know those answers and feel confident talking about them. Seems obvious, right? Unfortunately, it doesn't always happen. Jam-packed schedules, new product launches, complex portfolios, and risk avoidance tend to get in the way.

In fact, when I ask salespeople why they aren't pushing new products as part of the solution, some of their responses include:

- "I don't understand it."

- "I don't think this is what our customers need."

- "It creates friction in my sales process."

- "I get paid very little on it compared to the other products in my toolbox."

With a list like that, no wonder they aren't selling it!

As someone who sells for a living and works closely with salespeople to create enablement programs, I totally get it. We would always rather talk about what we know best and what we believe in. We don't want to endanger our reputations or potentially lose sales because we don't have a firm grasp on what we're selling.

It's Risk Avoidance 101. We avoid talking about a product we don't completely understand to avoid the risk of losing credibility.

Early in my career, I was conducting a discovery call with a prospect who asked me a fundamental question about one of my products. I couldn't answer it. I stuttered, then rambled, and felt like a fool. I wasn't surprised when the prospect ghosted me after that. It was a hard—but important—lesson to learn.

Shawn Taylor, member of the Purdue University Board of Trustees and the Noodles & Company Board of Directors, echoes this sentiment about preparation:

> One of the things that I assess immediately when somebody's trying to sell me something is, have you done your homework? Are you prepared? Do you know your product? And if you don't, stop wasting my time because I shouldn't have to ask you basic questions about the

product. I expect you to know the economics of your solution and sell me the benefits of it.[1]

Knowing the product well is a nonnegotiable part of the sales process. When we can't articulate what our product does, we also run the risk of eroding any trust with our clients.

In this chapter, I'll share two ways to increase your product knowledge and achieve greater success.

1. UNDERSTAND THE FUNDAMENTALS

Knowledge is everything. It's not just about being able to repeat the 30,000-foot overview statements or some canned talking points. I'm referring to next-level preparation and knowing your stuff.

These are the foundational questions we should be able to answer about our products so we can sell value as it pertains to our buyers. Let's explore each one.

What Is It?

The message here is simple: We need to know our products or services. I always followed that rule as a salesperson and emphasize that when working with other sellers. Employing specific strategies dramatically ramps up product knowledge:

- **Expand product fluency by talking with top sales performers.** Schedule time for conversations with people who have already been selling the product successfully. Listen closely, record the discussions, and transcribe notes.

Find common themes and identify areas where their passion really shines through. Ask to observe some of their sales calls, and when you do, pay attention to how they position the product and what language they use. What words or phrases resonate with the customer? What features and benefits seem to generate the most interest with potential buyers?

- **Check the facts.** I can't stand it when people stretch the truth about what their products really do. And I'm guessing your buyers don't like that either. That means we need clarity on what our products do—and don't do. No wiggle room there. If we get it wrong, our credibility is on the line.

    So, when learning about your products, take the trust but verify approach. Don't be shy about checking the validity of any claims before repeating them to a prospect.

- **Read customer testimonials.** Your organization likely has endorsements that highlight the reasons why customers selected your solution, as well as case studies that describe their buying journeys. Study those resources to help you understand their points of view and rationale for partnering with your company.

- **Check with the enablement team for product training.** If your organization has designed training programs, reach out to members of the enablement team and explain your learning goals. They should be able to direct you to the appropriate training materials if they exist.

- **Use the product.** I realize this may not be possible in every circumstance—like if you sell high-end surgical tools to a hospital's neurology department. But if you're selling an SaaS solution that you can use in your own role, there's no excuse for *not* being a user.

When we bring our own "customer experience" to the conversation, that shows buyers we believe in our product and the benefits it offers. That's powerful!

In one of my sales positions, I pulled up the solution on my iPad so the customer could see how I used it. Speaking from a user perspective, I talked with conviction, authenticity, and passion about the problems it solved for me while demonstrating that the solution could do the same for them.

Here's the big takeaway from all of that. If we aren't using our products to solve the same problems our customers are facing, why would we expect our customers to use them?

Whom Does It Target?

It's a fact: *We can't be everything to everyone.* So be crystal clear about the intended audience for your products or services.

What Is the Corporate Buyer Profile?

- What industries or organizations need the solution you're selling?

- What companies would be the best fit for your product?

- What is the typical size of an organization that could benefit (number of employees, market share, revenue)?

- Where are those organizations located?

What Is the Actual Buyer Persona?

- What common titles are held by the typical decision makers for your product?

- Where do they usually fall on the organization chart?

- What are their general roles and responsibilities?

- What do their typical business days look like?

Although many things change—our economy, culture, technology, product innovations—one thing remains the same in B2B enterprise deals: *People buy from people, not companies.* To connect with and truly serve our customers, we have to get to know them—to put ourselves in their shoes.

When starting to sell sales kickoff (SKO) programs, the best thing I did was to participate in every aspect, from planning to implementation. I got involved in the content development process and even attended and worked at a lot of these events.

In the trenches with the enablement leaders, I experienced everything firsthand. The war room. The stress. The sleepless nights. The surprises and the obstacles. The wins and the losses. It gave me an up-close view of their challenges and an opportunity to learn how to speak their language.

This experience allowed me to design SKO programs that were highly relevant and perfectly tailored for my audiences, aligning my solution with their needs.

What Problems Does It Solve for Your Customers?

When learning about your product, take a customer-centric perspective. Stay focused on how it helps solve their business problems. How does it support achieving their goals?

It's easy to get sidetracked by the cool "bells and whistles" features the design team folded into the latest release. But if those additions aren't specifically linked to helping prospects solve real problems and reach their goals, those components shouldn't take the lead in sales discussions.

Make it a priority to know which parts of your solution will create an actual impact for your customers. What's the typical ROI for your buyers? What are the tangibles? Always look for problem-solving facts to share, not slick gimmicks or fluff.

What Are the Key Differentiators?

Customers generally have options in terms of product selection, including the passive choice to stick with the status quo. So, it is critical to prepare a concise, compelling answer to these questions from buyers:

- "How is your solution different from others?"
- "Why should I choose your product?"
- "Do I even need to change?"
- "Why do I need to change *now*?"

Above all else, be clear about your solution's differentiators and tie them directly to customer benefits. In other words, don't simply launch into a discussion about your product's features and functions. Competing with those checklists is a one-way ticket to becoming a commodity. Work to understand the features and benefits from your customer's perspective. Then define your differentiators in terms of how they can help customers run their businesses more efficiently.

If you're still struggling to identify the key differentiators for your product, take a closer look at previous deals you and your colleagues have won. Why did the customers say they chose your solution? Are they happy with that choice? How did you measure success? When there are patterns and common themes among those answers, you'll find the differentiators—and be able to tell whether they are sticking.

2. FIND THE PASSION FOR WHAT YOU'RE SELLING

No big surprise here: Products we believe in and are passionate about are easier to sell. But sometimes the passion is missing . . . and that's a problem.

Get Excited About Your Product

It's hard to muster the enthusiasm to sell something we aren't excited about. If we're not convinced, there's a good chance we aren't completely disguising our apathy in our sales meetings. Does that mean skipping over those products and focusing on the sure winners in our solution portfolio?

Not necessarily.

The first step is to find the root cause of your apathy. I've been in that situation, and the absence of passion is a huge roadblock. At one point, I had an issue selling a solution because I thought it was over-priced. Every time I lost a deal, I told myself the pricing was the culprit. Through self-reflection and feedback, I eventually realized my lack of success had much less to do with the price point and much more to do with my attitude. My mindset was getting in the way. What a wake-up call!

In response, I had to fight to find my passion for the product. First, I hit reset and objectively looked at the value my solution could bring to my buyers. I looked more closely at customer success stories and uncovered some fresh differentiators I'd missed. By removing my biases and focusing on the business outcomes the product could generate, I brought a new attitude to my sales calls—and that resulted in more deals in my pipeline.

Factor in the Overall Customer Experience

If you're in search of sales passion, keep in mind that you're selling more than just the end product. The customer experience matters, and you can control what that overall package looks like with the value-added service you provide.

Yes, our products need to work well and deliver on promises. That's a given. But in its State of the Connected Customer survey (second edition), Salesforce Research found that "80% of customers say the experience a company provides is as important as its products or services."[2]

That begs the question: What kind of customer experience are we delivering?

Discuss the post-sale experience your company can offer and emphasize the differentiators with your prospect. These might include onboarding or training courses, support services or help desks, team availability, additional tools or resources, and access to expertise. In addition, highlight the ease of doing business with you—your quick response, detailed follow-up, insights, and partnership approach.

All those differentiators add perceived value to the product. If your actual product has a few drawbacks, compensate by delivering an exceptional customer experience.

Recognize When It's Time to Move On

There's no sugarcoating this one. Sometimes you make every effort to find passion for selling your product, and it's just not there. You adjust your mindset, study the success stories, and focus on the benefits of the customer experience. And still . . . nothing. This is tough for lots of sales reps, including me. Our competitive sides don't want to give up, even if we're miserable.

Maybe your hesitation about the product really stems from concerns about the company or your work environment. Is it a positive place to be? Or is the constant negativity weighing you down? Do you trust the people you work for? Would you describe the corporate climate as collaborative or cutthroat? Maybe struggling to sell the product is just the tip of the iceberg.

Sadly, one more thing must be said. If your candid assessment of the organization turns up hints of deceit or any shady operations, do yourself a favor and walk away. Don't risk your reputation as a sales professional long term, not to mention the potential legal troubles you could face, by associating with a company that is short on honesty and integrity.

The good news? There will always be admirable companies searching for great salespeople who know their products well and truly believe in them.

ESSENTIAL TAKEAWAYS

- Understand the fundamentals of your product by talking with and observing top sales performers, reading customer testimonials and case studies, taking full advantage of enablement tools, and using the product yourself (if applicable).

- Be crystal clear about your intended audience (buyer profile and buyer persona).

- Take a customer-centric perspective and stay focused on how your product can help solve your customers' business problems.

- Know your solution's differentiators and tie them directly to customer benefits.

- Find the passion for what you're selling and support that by delivering an exceptional customer experience.

- Be willing to make a change if your lack of passion to sell the product stems from a bad work environment.

CHAPTER
5

Build Your
Social Presence

In 2008, I was just finishing work on my PhD when I landed a consulting gig that led me to enterprise sales. To be honest, I was a big nerd. I wanted to sell, but the only thing I knew how to do was research. In retrospect, that might have been a blessing in disguise.

My first encounter with social selling began when I was targeting a large company. I needed to identify several key players in the organization so I could reach out to them and somehow convince them to meet with me. I had no idea where to start.

Business networking sites were new to me then, and I initially thought of them as mostly job-search resources. Things changed when I accidentally discovered the free "filter" functionality on LinkedIn. I remember entering a company name and being surprised to see that one of my acquaintances used to work there. Even more interesting? I could see some of his connections.

That was my first *wow* moment with social selling—the ability to seamlessly uncover hidden contacts that were, sometimes, closer than I imagined.

I immediately reached out to my contact and told him what I was working on to see if he could connect me with the right people. He described one colleague who seemed to fit my buyer persona and offered to make the introductions. The minute he told me this person's name, I quickly checked him out on LinkedIn. Bingo! There it was: everything I wanted to know about his current role and background. I could even message him, right there.

That connection eventually led to a lucrative deal—and I was hooked! Ever since then, I have used social selling as a research tool to identify and connect with prospects, build relationships with existing customers, and move deals toward a close.

For those of you who crave data, you're probably clamoring for hard facts that prove the impact of social selling. These stats are for you:

- At least 46 percent of B2B buyers are using social media at the very early stages of the buying journey; 40 percent use it in the middle; and 35 percent use it at the late stage of the sales process.[1]

- Sixty-eight percent of B2B buyers prefer to research online (up 15 percent from three years ago), and close to 62 percent use digital content to finalize their vendor lists.[2]

- Just over 92 percent of B2B buyers noted they are "more likely to purchase a product or service if they have been able to read a trusted review about it."[3]

Your digital presence is the constant backdrop for everything else you do to make sales. It's often the first place prospects encounter you, and it represents an ongoing line of communication to help grow and sustain your relationships over time. That's why I'm talking about social selling first and giving it its own chapter.

I have used social selling as a tool to land quite a few deals, and I train reps to integrate it with other prospecting channels. My approach is based on my experience identifying patterns and best practices, my own and third-party research, and my observations of other top performers who've successfully used social selling. This chapter includes my techniques and tips for getting the most out of this channel.

AUDIT YOUR DIGITAL FOOTPRINT

Before dedicating yourself to implementing a social selling strategy, you need to know what your digital footprint currently looks like. In today's world, how you show up online is an important part of making a first impression on potential buyers.

If you're trying to land an initial meeting with what could become your biggest customer, know up front that your contact person at the company is going to check you out in advance by either typing your name into a search engine or going directly to your LinkedIn profile. They prequalify leads, too! Are you legitimate or will this be a waste of time?

While not breaking news, it's still very important. In a 2018 blog interview, analysts at global market research company Forrester noted buyers are likely giving us the virtual "once over" before they agree to our call or meeting.[4] A LinkedIn study also claims that 49 percent of buyers research their reps in advance on their platform.[5]

So what happens when our buyers engage in this kind of online reconnaissance?

According to sales software company HubSpot, 75 percent of people never click past the initial page of search results,[6] so those top hits really need to count. Are you putting your best virtual foot forward, so to speak? What kind of image are you projecting? Does it align with your professional strengths and competencies? Is there anything out there that could undermine your credibility? Or is anything missing? LinkedIn reports that "50% of buyers will avoid reps with incomplete profiles."[7]

If you haven't done it lately, it's time to see how you show up online. Conduct a digital audit using the steps that follow.

Google Your Name

Set your browser to incognito or private mode and log out of your Google accounts. Then type in your name. This will show you what your prospects or buyers see without being impacted by your search history.

Review the First Page of Search Results

What things show up and what do they say about you? Your social media accounts likely appear at the top. If there are concerning posts or platforms that need to be addressed, you have several options:

- Remove them—or ask for help from the webmaster to do it.

- If you can't remove them, push out new content so the problematic items drop to the second or third pages of a Google search on your name.

Don't forget to click on the Images tab, too. If there are pictures you don't want buyers or prospects to see, remove them.

Proactively Monitor Your Online Presence

Besides repeating the Google search and review every quarter, using Google alerts is another free way to get a valuable heads-up when something online could impact your ability to sell.

Set up Google alerts to notify you any time your name appears on the internet. That's an interesting exercise for several reasons. Obviously, you want to know when your name is mentioned so you can respond appropriately. But what if the mentions that show up are about someone else with the same name? Click on the News section to learn more and get the facts.

It's helpful to be aware of those potential mix-ups in case a customer mentions it—or even to be proactive with clarification and a little humor:

> Nice to meet you! I'm Jason Brown. And just so you know, I'm not the Jason Brown who's been in the news lately fighting the IRS about back taxes. I'm a different guy—and I'm all paid up with Uncle Sam!

DEVELOP A TARGETED SOCIAL SELLING STRATEGY

With your digital audit complete, move into planning mode with a laser focus on creating a highly efficient social selling strategy.

No one in sales has time to waste. When using social platforms in our sales approach, we want a reasonable ROI. Time is money! So how can we get the most impact from our social selling efforts? The following three steps are helpful.

Be Clear About Your Goals

Identify the purpose for using a social media platform such as LinkedIn. Do you want to land new customers, nurture existing relationships, expand business within your current accounts, or pursue all three simultaneously? Or are you looking for a new job? Be clear about what you're trying to accomplish. Without that, your strategy and execution suffer.

Know Your Audience and Their Social Media Habits

Based on your goals, pinpoint the target audience you want to reach. If your goal is to land new business, get specific about your corporate buyer profile and ideal buyer persona. The more focused you are, the easier it is to find customers who align with those targets and represent opportunities for greater sales.

Then take time to understand them and, more importantly, their social media habits. Which platforms do they use? What are their go-to resources? Follow your buyers, show up where they are, and differentiate yourself so you stand out from the crowd. That tried-and-true strategy never fails.

Full disclosure, I'm not associated with LinkedIn. But for many in B2B sales, LinkedIn is the most direct way to create ongoing opportunities for interaction with current and potential buyers. LinkedIn's research even supports that, showing that 80 percent of their members drive business decisions.[8] For that reason, LinkedIn is referred to throughout the book. But if your buyers are on another platform, find out where they are and make sure they see you there. Out of sight, out of mind!

Once you've figured out where you need to be, pay attention to your buyers' social media habits. What do they post? What do they comment on? What do they seem to care about? Look at the groups and hashtags they follow so you can go where they are and understand what's relevant to them. Learn to speak their language.

Be Patient

Just because a potential buyer accepts your connection request doesn't mean you should immediately send an email pitching your product. Generic pitches don't work. And, even worse, they can (and likely will) annoy your potential buyer.

I'll admit, this is a tough one for those of us who aren't patient, but it's true. Social selling is more of a marathon than a sprint. Recognize that this process is most successful with ongoing engagement over time and integration with other channels. Adopt a methodical approach that allows you to develop familiarity. Above all, know your strategy and keep moving forward at a steady pace.

REFINE YOUR ONLINE POSITIONING

Based on your defined objectives, revisit your pertinent social media profiles. In this case, I'm referring to your LinkedIn profile. Focus on refining how you position yourself there. Let's consider some tips for doing that.

Use a Current Photo

It's awkward when you go to appointments or get on Zoom calls with prospects, and they can't recognize you from your profile picture. If your photo is outdated (or you don't have one), it's time to get a quality headshot. That's a must for salespeople—particularly in social selling.

Former LinkedIn product manager Aaron Bronzan explained in a blog post that adding a photo makes your profile "seven times more likely to be found in searches."[9] LinkedIn content marketer Lydia Abbot agrees and shared research that indicates you'll get 14 times more views with a picture than without one.[10]

Create a Compelling Headline

As you write your profile headline, make it client facing.[11] Don't just include your title. Give them more! What would capture your prospects' attention? What's the hook? Forget the cheesy or exaggerated and focus on meaningful words for them based on their goals and challenges. When you strategically design this opening phrase, you'll have a much better chance of pulling people in and intriguing them enough to read your summary.

Craft a Summary That Resonates with Your Prospects

Think of your profile summary—the *About* section—as part of your sales prospecting strategy and an extension of your headline, like the body of an outreach email. That's a different approach than including a couple of paragraphs about how great you are at your job. Instead, focus on your buyers. Put yourself in their position, tapping into the mindset that captures their priorities. When you start writing, describe your credentials in a way that demonstrates how you can help to solve their problems.

Another tip: Present yourself as an individual.[12] Use the first-person ("I") narrative, along with a conversational tone. Incorporate stories to connect and be remembered. Make sure your summary is concise, clear, and easy to follow. When prospects finish reading this introductory section, they should get the impression you are personable and understand their world.

Compare the difference in impact between the introductory summary statements that follow. While full summaries might be several thousand characters, these phrases show you the diverse perspectives:

Self-centered (vs.) Customer-focused

Focused on the seller's abilities and achievements: "World-class salesperson; exceeded quotas in the last 7 quarters; added 2 top-tier clients in FY 2021; received district award for Top Salesperson in 2022."

Versus...

Focused on understanding and meeting the needs of customers: "I'm passionate about serving midsize to large organizations in the IT industry, supporting their mission-critical applications with a goal of zero downtime. As someone who's been in your shoes, I know what it means when systems go down and everyone is frantically calling you. I understand the impact in terms of lost revenue, drops in productivity, poor employee morale, unhappy customers, and damaged reputations (for the people involved and the company). I'm fully committed to avoiding those negative outcomes."

Be sure to include a call to action with your complete contact information. If you have a current photo, compelling headline, and knockout summary that really speaks to them, make it easy for them to reach out.

Complete Your Profile with the Same Client Focus

Finish out the rest of your social media profile with the same emphasis on customer value. For instance, update the descriptions of your roles and responsibilities in terms of how you provide service for your clients. Be specific about the benefits you can offer. Don't hesitate to include customer recommendations. If a prospect is reviewing your profile, the words of highly satisfied customers can be extremely powerful.

ENGAGE AND ADD VALUE

At this point, you've optimized your digital presence for social selling. Now you get to the heart of the process—interacting on an ongoing basis and engaging with prospects on a deeper level.

Be Strategic About Your Chosen Content

Use what you know about current and potential buyers to identify topics genuinely important to them. Post information that is helpful, surprising, or thought-provoking. How can you add value for them through your content?

Besides providing your own content that's relevant to prospects, build in some variety by selectively sharing content from others that you admire and respect. In those cases, don't just write, "Love this!" or "Great post!" Summarize the content you share. Explain why it resonated with you and why you felt compelled to pass it along.

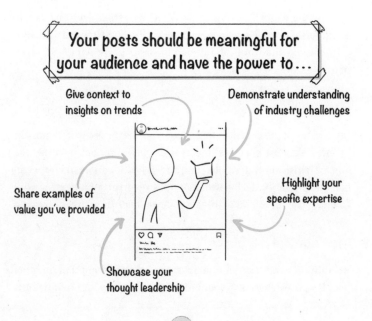

Your posts should be meaningful for your audience and have the power to...

Give context to insights on trends

Demonstrate understanding of industry challenges

Share examples of value you've provided

Highlight your specific expertise

Showcase your thought leadership

To identify great content, make a strategic list of potential post topics that would be meaningful for your audience and have the power to:

- Demonstrate your understanding of specific industry challenges.

- Give context to the insights on trends you provide to your prospects.

- Highlight your expertise in a given area and the benefits that creates for buyers.

- Share examples of the value you've added for other buyers.

- Showcase your thought leadership as it pertains to your buyers.

Vet these topics by asking: "So what? Why should my buyers care about this? How will it help them in their job/role? How will this influence the way they think about their business or my company, products, and value?"

Post Regularly

Beyond the strategy of deciding *what* to post is the issue of frequency. To effectively use social selling in your sales approach, you need to engage consistently. It's not a "one and done." It's about having a regular cadence and sticking with it. Putting recurring reminders in your calendar can be helpful so this effort doesn't fall through the cracks.

Interact Deliberately

In addition to adding content, invest the time to comment on other people's posts (especially your prospects) and make sure your name is showing up regularly throughout the feed. That process could include congratulating someone on a recent achievement, posing an interesting question, offering insights, or just expressing appreciation for a post you found valuable.

Focus on Connection

Here's some advice that you might find unexpected: Don't be afraid to show your human side.[13] It's perfectly fine—even preferable—to show up as an individual on social platforms. As I've mentioned before: People build relationships with other people, not companies. By sharing an occasional tidbit about your life, you add new layers and textures to your online persona. Even better, you may be providing your prospects with another possible connection point or some common ground that makes you more relatable.

In his research, Dr. Robert Cialdini, author of *Influence: Science and Practice*, found that someone is more likely to influence you if there are similarities between the two of you.[14] That's a great lesson in sales!

Here's an example to illustrate the strength of that concept.

I've been a runner since I was a kid. Throughout my youth and adult life, I always ran with earbuds. I'm obsessed with optimizing my time. Why just exercise when you can also listen to music, a book, or an interesting podcast?

One day, on a whim, I decided to run without the earbuds, and I discovered something fascinating: My brain was strangely productive. Being unplugged seemed to help me generate new ideas, find solutions that had been evading me, or just connect the dots for an *aha!* moment. It was quite remarkable.

I wondered if that experience might provide a unique connection point on social media, so I posted about it on LinkedIn, and the topic generated lively engagement. Several of my contacts and potential buyers had gotten the exact same results, which led to some interesting discussions. This conversation starter helped my prospects see me in a different light—as a human who does more than just sell and someone willing to share an experience in hopes it might help others. Creating that new connection point allowed me to grow several key relationships.

TURN ENGAGEMENT INTO A SALES CONVERSATION

If you've consistently and patiently followed your social selling strategy, you've probably established a strong foundation for engaging with your potential buyers.

It's time to transform that engagement into an actual sales conversation. Choose your timing carefully and identify a specific reason to meet with the potential buyer. Use what you've learned from your social media interactions to make a persuasive, customized case for scheduling a meeting.

You may discover your ongoing virtual relationships give you a significant advantage to get your proverbial foot in the door.

When I started my business, I didn't have a lot of name recognition online. And although I had worked in the sales industry for a long time and was good at my job, I failed when it came to building my own digital brand. Honestly, I didn't think I needed to.

I quickly realized that was an incorrect assumption.

My inner graduate student with a passion for research took over. I started interviewing thought leaders to find out more about sales best practices and talked to executives in what I anticipated would be part of my target audience. Using that information, I developed a social selling strategy to increase my virtual brand awareness.

Part of my strategy was to begin a blog on LinkedIn, and I was so grateful that my colleagues and friends were willing to take time and support my posts. Slowly but surely, my audience started noticing my content. Through associations with the amazing sales leaders I knew and interviewed, my blog gained traction with an increase in "likes" and comments.

I regularly reviewed my post analytics and researched the people who had engaged, looking for those who fit my buyer personas. Any time someone left a comment, I promptly replied with added value. And that's how it happened!

A potential buyer liked one of my posts, and I responded with an insightful comment. Then I quickly did some research to understand more about this person and her role in the company. During that process, I read one of her posts that authentically resonated with me.

When I sent her a request to connect on LinkedIn, I mentioned her post and explained why it had caught my attention. I weaved in a number of statements that showed I understood her business and some of the challenges she might be facing. I also shared a few targeted insights. That personalized approach worked, and she accepted my request.

From that point on, I started showing up regularly in my prospect's LinkedIn newsfeed. Plus, I learned more about her business from her posts and identified opportunities to add value. As the familiarity increased, we engaged with each other's content on a consistent basis. It didn't happen overnight, but our virtual relationship began to grow.

A few months later, I sent her a customized email requesting a meeting. I provided a compelling reason why that investment of her time would be to her advantage. Thankfully, she accepted—and we identified a need that led us to work together soon after that.

Social selling is a process and an ongoing effort, but it can be a brilliant way to prime the pump for sales success. To use it effectively, be sure to have a laser-focused strategy and a targeted approach to reaching your prospects and customers. Then, take every chance you get to engage with your contacts and add value for them. That consistency in presence and providing relevant information will open up more productive interactions as you move through the sales cycle.

ESSENTIAL TAKEAWAYS

- Audit your digital footprint to ensure your professional strengths align with your online presence.

- Develop a targeted social selling strategy that clarifies your goals and your intended audience.

- Refine your online positioning and presentation to appeal to your prospects.

- Deliberately add content that's relevant for your targets and engage with them regularly.

- Transform that engagement into actual sales conversations by making a compelling case to schedule a meeting.

CHAPTER

6

Be Diligent About Prospecting

How do you feel about rejection? Do you enjoy being ghosted, ignored, or hung up on? Of course not! None of us do. In fact, according to HubSpot, 40 percent of sales reps say prospecting is the most challenging part of the job.[1]

I agree. But prospecting is also absolutely critical for success in sales.

Based on my experience, one reason for not meeting quotas is not having enough opportunities in the sales pipeline. In other words, we're not prospecting regularly. We make it to the end of the quarter—that last month when we're counting on a few more deals to land. Then, unexpectedly, one of those deals gets pushed two months out. Ouch. That's when desperation sets in, and we start feverishly prospecting. It's rushed and haphazard. We're basically setting ourselves up to fail.

Initially, I thought prospecting would be fairly easy. How hard could it be to get one person to agree to meet with me?

Reality quickly slapped me in the face.

Despite spending hours making phone calls, leaving voice messages, and sending emails, my response rate wasn't great. Keep in mind this was before we had tools like LinkedIn Sales Navigator to help quickly create automated lists.

One morning, I was particularly frustrated by the long parade of rejection. My Sent folder contained dozens of prospecting emails that seemed absolutely worthless. What was I doing wrong?

I printed out all those emails and divided them into two piles: Response and No Response. Needless to say, the No Response pile was quite hefty. But after comparing the piles, I noticed some subtle differences.

The No Response emails were more generic and formal. They included brochure language and were sent to people in human resource roles. The Response emails were more friendly and conversational. They were customized and addressed to people in sales and marketing-related areas, which are more aligned with my buyer personas. Those were interesting insights! And they meant I needed to go back to the drawing board.

I started spending more time identifying the right targets and making sure my emails were reaching them. I also worked on customizing my communications. With that new approach, things started to change.

To this day, I remember coming back from lunch and seeing my voice message light on. I pushed the button to listen while walking to my next meeting. "Hello, my boss received your email this morning, and he'd like to schedule some time with you to discuss it."

Years later, I can still hear that woman's voice (and my subsequent scream: "*Yes!*"). It was a turning point in my career. And since then, by following the best practices in this chapter, I've regularly landed meetings with top executives of global organizations. It's all about the process and discipline.

Let's look at each step involved in prospecting.

PROSPECT REGULARLY

Like it or not, prospecting is an essential part of the sales process. Highly targeted. Consistent. Ongoing.

So how can you make sure that prospecting remains the constant fuel source for your sales success?

Set Aside Recurring Time on Your Calendar

Consider prospecting a nonnegotiable priority. It's easy to get busy and fill that time with something that feels more urgent at that moment. But remember that investing time is critical to build and maintain a healthy pipeline.

Minimize Distractions to Improve Focus

Keep your door closed and your digital devices off or silenced. Keep your head in the game. When busy prospecting, I reduce interruptions by letting people know I'm temporarily unavailable if they see a closed door, a "do not disturb" sign, or a designated light.

Consider Prospects' Email Behaviors and Time Zones

Some of my potential buyers tend to check their email before or after the standard workday. That prompted me to adjust my prospecting strategy and include some outreach in the early morning and evening hours. By doing this, my response rate increased. Try experimenting with your own clients, prospecting at different times and tracking results. You may discover timing is everything.

BUILD AND NURTURE YOUR NETWORK

Ask any salesperson. It's always easier to call on a potential prospect who was referred to you by one of their colleagues or a mutual friend than to cold-call someone. It's also more effective because the initial connection gives you instant credibility.

That explains the saying: "Your network is your net worth." Research published in the *Journal of Applied Psychology* backs that up, showing that networking is a key driver behind "salary growth over time" and career satisfaction.[2]

Think about your network of professional and personal contacts as a living, breathing entity. By actively feeding and nurturing it, you'll unlock the power behind those connections to develop relationships, identify new opportunities, and get in front of the right people at the right time. If you let it languish, you'll be making the sales process much harder.

To build and nurture your network, follow these guidelines.

Go Where Your Prospects Are

It's hard to maintain connections if you aren't "connecting." Do your potential buyers attend local trade association meetings or national conferences? Do they belong to virtual groups or have a heavy presence on certain social media platforms? Will they be at specific trade shows or networking events? Leverage those opportunities by showing up wherever they are.

On a related note, be proactive about making *new* contacts. This is particularly important since Covid-19 arrived on the scene. Not surprisingly, research from *Harvard Business Review* found that professional and personal networks shrunk by nearly 16 percent during the pandemic.[3] It's clear there are benefits to getting out there and meeting some new people (or reconnecting with previous contacts).

Create Mutually Beneficial Relationships

Having hundreds of names in email address books doesn't equate with a thriving network. The goal is to build *meaningful* connections that translate into actual business relationships. In sales, that means staying in contact with the people and demonstrating we're interested in them as human beings—and that doesn't just apply to potential buyers. Save the sales pitch for later and develop the relationships first.

Keep in mind that these relationships need to be a two-way street. Working to build networks means giving as much as (or more than) we take. Add value and collaborate.

Ask: "What could I do to support these people in their success?" The answer might be sharing a link to a recent article, suggesting a book they might enjoy, offering a pertinent white paper, making an introduction, or simply commenting on a post about one of their recent wins. (How often to reach out is addressed later in this chapter.)

Stay in Touch

If you haven't checked on some of your contacts lately, get in touch to ask what they've been up to. Even better, use that outreach as an opportunity to add value. Maybe you share some insights, provide a link to a relevant article, or pass along the contact information for someone you think they should know. When you follow up with them to reconnect, you'll be keeping the relationship alive until the time is right to move forward with the request for a sales meeting.

GO AFTER LOW-HANGING FRUIT

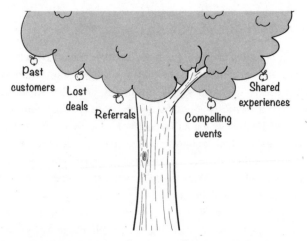

Prospecting doesn't have to involve starting from the beginning every time. If you know your target audience and are clear on their buyer personas, the leads you want may be closer than you think.

Past Customers

Maybe former satisfied clients moved to a different company, or perhaps you landed a new job. If you haven't had a conversation with past buyers lately, reach out. They already know you and your capabilities and may be the fastest route to your next deal.

This approach is what I call the path of least resistance because some trust has already been formed with these contacts, and trust is the secret sauce!

Lost Deals

Just because we don't make a sale with a customer doesn't mean giving up on the relationship. Sometimes the deal is lost because the product, budget, or timing simply didn't align. But if we have done our jobs and delivered value in every interaction, the prospects will remember us. On many occasions, I have reconnected with potential buyers who once said no and convinced them to say yes at a later date by adding value.

Referrals

Research from marketing intelligence firm IDC shows us that 76.2 percent of buyers prefer to work with vendors who have "been recommended to me by someone I know."[4] Yet how many of us really ask for referrals? The answer is, very few! If asking for referrals isn't part of your sales strategy, you may be missing an easy way to find the next deal. Here's how to do that:

- Ask your loyal customers to introduce you to their colleagues experiencing similar challenges. It's a simple request.

- Look through your LinkedIn connections for trusted colleagues and friends who might be willing to help you tap into their networks. If you have good relationships with them, they'll likely be happy to pass along some suggestions for potential references.

- Make it as easy as possible for people to introduce you to one of their contacts. Write an email they can customize and forward.

Compelling Events

Know what's happening in your clients' worlds. Is a new compliance requirement about to be enforced across their industry? Did they just lose a major customer? Is their biggest competitor about to launch a game-changing product? Did they acquire a new company? Did they fail to meet expectations this quarter? Was there a shakeup in top leadership?

When there's a compelling event, there's a sense of urgency for problem solving. By showing up with the right solution at that moment, the odds of winning the deal go way, way up.

Shared Experiences

Sometimes connecting with a potential buyer has nothing to do with our extensive knowledge or product quality. Instead, we may grab the prospect's attention because of an overlap in life experiences. We went to the same school. Support the same community nonprofit. Enjoy the same hobby. Have kids in the same class. "Sameness" provides a natural connection and instant rapport for building a great relationship. By following up with a compelling business reason to meet, those similarities can be leveraged to get an appointment.

The power of this technique was highlighted in a blog interview I conducted with the late Chris Townsend, the former chief revenue officer at CivicPlus and a former executive in the IT industry. "A while back, a rep pinged me on LinkedIn," Townsend explained. "He personalized the communications by mentioning my passion for coaching youth sports and said he coaches, too. I was more inclined to respond to him because he picked up on my passion and connected with me as a human. And it didn't take him much time to find that information—maybe seconds to scroll down on my LinkedIn profile and say, 'Oh, this guy's a youth coach.'"[5]

Now, was that common interest enough to land a deal? No. But it held the prospect's attention a bit longer and allowed him to discover that a meeting with the rep could add genuine value. The shared experience was the gateway to making a profitable connection.

What About the Sales Funnel?

As you may know, some companies' marketing departments support their sales teams with a highly structured, automated process called a sales funnel. The funnel is designed to transform prospects into loyal customers by exposing them to a series of targeted communications or "assets"—social media posts, case studies, white papers, demo videos, webinars, and more. A lot of these assets are also used by salespeople during prospecting to educate potential customers, add insights, and differentiate themselves.

If the funnel is successful, it results in greater sales by moving the audience through a defined cycle of engagement (awareness, interest, desire, action, retention, and advocacy). The shape of the process is often graphically depicted as a funnel, which is how it got the name.

Stages of a Sales Funnel

Awareness

Interest

Desire

Action

Retention

Advocacy

Note there are different approaches and opinions when it comes to funnels. Common questions involve who really owns the funnel (marketing or sales?), which assets are needed, and where they belong. Like the answer to many things, it depends.

While this book doesn't focus specifically on sales funnels (there are plenty out there from people who specialize in this area), here's the point I'd like to emphasize: the critical importance of *alignment between marketing and sales* throughout the process. Marketing might be physically creating the funnel assets, but salespeople specialize in understanding the objectives and challenges of potential customers. Their front-row perspective is essential for creating personalized messaging that is highly targeted and relevant to buyer personas.

So how can organizations ensure that continuity of thought? I recommend creating a *cross-functional advisory team* to guide the development of funnel assets. This could include sales colleagues, sales leaders, marketing leaders, enablement leaders, and content creators. With that deep collaboration, funnels are infinitely more successful and sales reps get an instant credibility boost that helps them stand out from their competition.

USE MULTIPLE CHANNELS

If you're actively building and strengthening your network, you're ahead of the game when it comes to communicating with your prospects and working to land discovery meetings. But the key to remaining visible is to use different channels to stay in touch—emails, phone calls, voicemail messages, and social media.

In a nutshell, exclusively using one channel limits potential.

Chorus by ZoomInfo (the company behind the top-rated conversation intelligence platform for sales teams) analyzed 35 million sales calls and reported some interesting statistics:[6]

- It takes sales reps 106 phone dials to get one scheduled meeting, and only 27 percent of those dials connect.[7]

- About 32 percent of those discovery meetings move into the late stages of the sales process.[8]

- Only 19 percent of those meetings end in a closed deal.[9]

Imagine what would happen if you integrated email, social media, phone calls, and voicemail into the mix. Based on my experience, it will help to increase the response rate as part of your follow-up strategy.

Is there a recommended sequence for using these different channels? It all depends on whom you ask and which audience you're targeting, so you'll need to see what works best for your situation. However, I can share the typical approach I use to integrate the channels for optimal results.

Social Media

My participation on social media platforms such as LinkedIn creates the framework for most of my prospecting and allows me to be a familiar face among my buyers and prospects. I regularly post content relevant to them and try to use the same hashtags they do.

Email

Once I have built virtual relationships and have a legitimate reason for reaching out, I develop a customized email to make contact and, hopefully, land a meeting. If I've done a good job with my social media, I won't be a total stranger when my email arrives.

After sending out prospecting emails, I follow up by checking recipients' LinkedIn profiles—an action that triggers a secondary contact they will notice. That combination of prospecting outreach helps to build familiarity.

Phone Calls and Voicemail Messages

Reaching out with a phone call bridges the gap between being a digital presence and a real person with a voice and emotions. This connection makes me more real with my prospects, even if I have to leave a voicemail message.

I make it a habit to follow up with emails that reference my phone call or voice message and include something of value. That helps my social media presence remain steady.

Inevitably, salespeople want to know how many times they should follow up with prospects. The answer to that depends on a variety of factors, including the buyer persona, the industry, and the sales cycle. While there isn't a magic number of interactions to recommend for effective prospecting, research by the productivity software company Yesware shows the first six touches using email and phone over a 14-day period are ranked as the most important.[10] This is based on analyzing 33 million email activities over three years. Additional touches are certainly warranted, and social media can help to increase the overall contacts. Generally speaking, the quality of interactions outweighs the quantity, so keep the emphasis on adding value while continuously testing, adjusting, and improving.

Other Channels

Beyond social media, email, and phone calls, there are additional channels you can integrate into your prospecting activities. For example, consider events where you might encounter some highly qualified potential customers. This might include trade shows, conferences, or industry gatherings. Be proactive about finding out who will attend, and try to schedule meetings with these prospects while you are there.

Another option is sending a handwritten note. Sometimes this old-fashioned touch is an excellent way to stand out in the sea of digital communications. We'll talk more about that later.

The first 6 touchpoints with a prospect over a 14-day period are the most important.

Source: Jenny Keohane, "The Best Sales Cadence Based on 33 Million Emails," *Yesware* (blog), May 3, 2022, https://www.yesware.com/blog/sales-cadence/.

PERSONALIZE YOUR OUTBOUND COMMUNICATIONS

Do you typically respond to generic emails and random phone calls? I'm guessing the answer is a hard no! Decision makers receive plenty of those every day, and they are a major turnoff.

As part of creating sales training programs, I regularly interview buyers to get their opinions about the prospecting behaviors of the sales reps who call on them. I consistently hear the same complaint: They hate generic, cut-and-paste communications. For multichannel prospecting to be successful, send messages that are relevant and grab the attention of potential buyers.

That means customizing. And to do that, you have to bring in the right research and incorporate it into outbound prospecting. In fact, according to LinkedIn's 2022 State of Sales report, the most successful salespeople tend to do the most research. Their findings showed that 82 percent of top performers say they "always" perform research before contacting a potential buyer, compared with only 49 percent of average sellers.[11]

As an example, Ash Shehata, senior vice president and CIO at AHMC Healthcare, Inc., shared this in May 2021 for one of my blog posts: "Let me give you an example of what won't get my attention," said Shehata. "I started my journey at AHMC in December. I've had 1,693 unsolicited emails and 874 unsolicited voicemails, of which I replied to zero. About 80 percent of the emails are generic, and they sound something like this: 'Hey, we help other healthcare organizations resolve all these challenges: security, implementation, all that.' I'm not interested in what you've done in other organizations that are different from ours or not even in the same sector. If you're going to bring examples, make them relevant to me."[12]

Customization is essential, but here's one additional piece of advice: It's easy to get sucked into the research process. One great article leads you to several interesting posts, and then you find relevant pictures and a wonderful white paper and a helpful video and . . . suddenly you've invested hours trying to dig up background information. Think about the costs versus the benefits and manage your time wisely.

Without putting some boundaries around research efforts, you may be losing time better spent reaching out and landing sales meetings.

We discussed customizing social media in Chapter 5, but let's look at guidelines for personalizing other outbound communications.

Customizing Emails

In an analysis of 20 million sales emails, Woodpecker—a B2B lead generation company—found that email reply rates doubled when outreach was personalized. The organization reported that the average response rate of advanced personalized emails was 17 percent versus 7 percent for nonpersonalized.[13]

For comparison, I recently conducted a prospecting campaign that involved sending more than 70 personalized emails to LinkedIn contacts that I either hadn't met or hadn't touched base with recently. To date, my response rate is 33.8 percent.

So, what's the secret? We have to capture the potential buyers' attention while being efficient with our time. Here are some helpful best practices:

- **Create an email template targeting a specific buyer persona.** This is particularly helpful if your ideal customers fall into a fairly narrow niche (industry, region, size). Remember that customization is essential but using an email template adds efficiency and gives you a head start on describing common challenges and initiatives. Those templates are also a great reminder to incorporate language that genuinely resonates with all prospects in that category.

- **Always begin the email with a name.** You'll probably lose the battle if you open with a generic greeting ("Hi!") or a reference to their title ("Dear Purchasing Manager"). Be specific and make sure you have the correct spelling of their names. Here's an extra tip: Use the first name only. If you include the first *and* last names in the greeting, your prospect may assume it's an automated message and hit Delete.

- **Pay attention to your subject line.** Exaggerations or deceptive phrases will land your email in the spam folder. Instead, craft something persuasive that draws from the customized information you'll be focusing on. Entice them to click and open.

- **Write from their perspective.** Based on what you know about your prospects' typical initiatives and challenges, create a list of common themes that may resonate with them. Be deliberate about weaving those topics into your email, demonstrating you understand their perspectives.

- **Make the first few sentences all about them.** Find a hook that shows you are paying attention to what's going on in their world:

    - Did the person publish something on LinkedIn that compelled you to reach out?

    - Did the person speak at a conference about a topic that resonated with you?

    - Did they just launch a new product?

    - Did they recently post their financials?

    - Did they receive an award or reach an important milestone?

- **Explain why you're reaching out.** Give them the reasons you're contacting them and describe why it's relevant for their goals and objectives.

- **Share something of value.** What can you offer a prospect that proves your intention to help them by adding value? This might include your insights, a pertinent resource, an introduction to someone else who could support them, or even your time.

- **Include a call to action without being pushy.** A prospecting email isn't the place to ask for the sale. The goal is to nail down an appointment.

Research from Gong (the company behind the top-rated revenue intelligence platform for B2B sales teams) indicates that salespeople are more effective when they position outreach as a request to know whether someone is interested in learning more about a certain topic.[14] The second most effective technique is suggesting a specific time for a meeting with the prospect, followed by an open-ended request to get together in the near future.

I typically use a combination of these approaches: gauging interest *and* recommending a day and time for the meeting, while asking them to suggest alternatives if that doesn't work. I'm providing an adapted sample of an outreach email I've used in prospecting for my sales enablement services.

CUSTOMIZED OUTREACH EMAIL: A SAMPLE

Hi Greg,

Congratulations on adding several new hospital systems, including the most recent one in Detroit; hiring a new CMO and CRO; adding more than 60 new sellers to the sales organization; and making it to the *Inc. 5000* list for three straight years. I also read that your company's growth strategy includes some potentially significant acquisitions. All of this compelled me to reach out and start a conversation.

When an organization is experiencing this type of growth, questions typically arise in these three areas:

- How can I be sure my current sales reps and new hires are the right fit for the company? *(reducing turnover rate and associated costs)*

- How can I maintain a dynamic sales process that is client-centric? *(increasing the number of reps making quota)*

- How do I enable my sales reps with the right content and training? *(expanding sales enablement tools to measurably increase sales)*

If you're interested in hearing how we helped other firms address some of these challenges, I'd love to set up a call or meet for coffee. Are you available on August 9 at 10 a.m. CST? If you're busy then, let me know other times that work best for you.

Take care,
Rana

Customizing Calls

I'm not a natural cold caller. I used to get so nervous my voice would shake and, secretly, I'd pray they wouldn't answer. Just like any skill that requires upleveling, I had to work on it, change my mindset, get help, and commit to regular practice. Sometimes it took a lot of discipline, but I used to sit in my office, door closed, with the goal to make a certain number of prospect calls—and a commitment to stay there until I finished.

Over the years, I have refined the structure of my calls by testing what works (and what doesn't), reading research studies, and implementing best practices. I'd recommend the same for you. Continuously test and adjust your call process to identify the sweet spot for your audience.

Here are some cold-calling tips to personalize your conversations and help you feel more confident. I've followed these guidelines for years and continue to see research that supports their validity:[15]

- **Greeting.** Start by saying the prospect's name. In my first college job as a bank teller, I remember watching the CEO walk around every morning and greet people by their names—customers and employees alike. People loved it! When I asked him why, he said, "Rana, a person's name is music to their ears."

  That wasn't just a brilliant observation. Research actually shows that hearing our names evokes a distinct brain activity.[16] Scientists also observed similar brain patterns with a male patient in a persistent vegetative state when his name was spoken, in contrast with another name.[17] Conscious or not, we love to hear our names.

Addressing people by their names is like giving them an instant "buzz" that makes them feel good. And when they feel good, they're much more likely to listen to what we have to say. Don't skip this step! Acknowledge your prospects and get their attention by using their names at the very beginning.

- **Introduction.** Clearly state your name and the name of your organization. It shows credibility and indicates that you're legit.

- **Purpose.** Explain the reason you're calling and make sure you customize it up front by integrating relevant research from the person's posts, comments, and company updates.

From a scientific perspective, research shows the power of the word "because" in getting people to comply with your request. Ellen Langer of Harvard University with Arthur Blank and Benzion Chanowitz of The Graduate Center at City University of New York published their findings from a classic study in the 1978 *Journal of Personality and Social Psychology*. Their goal was to test the psychology of asking for favors.[18]

As people were in line to use a copy machine, they were asked to let another person use it first. When the person didn't give a reason why he or she wanted to cut in, the success rate was around 60 percent. But if this person gave any type of reason at all, the people in line agreed 94 percent of the time. They concluded that presenting a reason increased the chance of compliance, even if the reason was random or flimsy.[19]

Research by Gong found similar results with sales. Cold callers who state the purpose for calling have more than two times the success rate of those who fail to provide a reason.[20]

As you describe the purpose of your call, make it obvious you've done your homework and have tried to understand their business.

- **Value.** Based on the reason for your call, share insights that add value for your prospects. What are you seeing in the marketplace that might resonate with them? What is your value proposition? Could you talk about success stories of working with similar customers?

- **Call to action.** If you've offered your prospects a compelling "because" statement, shared insights, and piqued their interest, they'll want to know more. But don't try to tell them everything over the phone. The goal is to get an appointment. Sell the meeting, not the product.

  If they agree, ask for an email address, and send a calendar invitation immediately after the call before you are forgotten.

Customizing Voicemail Messages

Researchers at Chorus found that 90 percent of cold calls end up in a voicemail message.[21] That's not a bad thing, as long as you're prepared. When you get the opportunity to record a message to your prospect, you're humanizing your communications by attaching a voice. That says a lot about you to the listeners. In fact, the human voice can communicate 24 different emotions that connect people in unique ways.[22]

The process is similar to that of the cold call, but you won't have time to collect your thoughts while the other person is speaking. Be ready. Be aware of your tone of voice, pitch, volume, and pace. Customize! Be specific but concise, leaving your name, your company name, the reason for your call, and your contact information. Let them know you'll follow up with an email.

FOLLOW UP

Even world-class salespeople have to circle back multiple times with prospects before they get a meeting. However, how many of us really do that? And I don't mean a single follow-up. I'm talking about multiple follow-up contacts and adding value *every time*.

In case following up isn't your favorite part of the sales process, you're not alone.

Do a Google search on the phrase "sales follow-up statistics," and you'll find a range of abysmal percentages of reps that are actually taking the initiative to stay in touch with their prospects. For example, Superoffice, a CRM software company, studied 1,000 organizations and "found that less than 3% of all companies send a follow-up email to their prospects or customers."[23]

Without circling back in a methodical way, leads grow cold and potential buyers move on. To avoid that loss, make follow-up a consistent part of your sales process.

Persistence Is Often Rewarded

If you've invested the time to identify the right potential buyer, engaged on social platforms, customized your message, and reached out to get an appointment, don't give up! I'm not suggesting that you become a crazy stalker, but be patient with the process and remember that not getting a response doesn't mean no. People are busy, and the arrival of your email may have coincided with the launch of a big initiative or a looming deadline for your potential buyer.

While I haven't seen a consensus for the perfect number of follow-up contacts in my readings and my experience working with reps, I generally follow the science that says salespeople need at least four touches to make an impact. Some studies indicate more than eight. Adjust your expectations accordingly.

Remind yourself: *I haven't heard from her, but I've only followed up twice so far. I need to stay the course and follow my cadence. I'm not giving up too early!*

Even if a prospect does say no, it might just mean "not yet." According to conversation rate optimization experts at Invesp, 60 percent of customers say no four times before saying yes.[24]

Speed of Response Is a Differentiator

Consistent, customized, multichannel prospecting will put you in the position for success. The deciding factor? How you handle the leads that emerge from your hard work. Because time is of the essence!

In a survey sponsored by Zendesk, a service-first CRM company, researchers asked 1,044 US consumers about their buying habits. The results clearly show that speed matters—with 89 percent reporting that "a quick response to an initial inquiry is important when deciding which company to buy from."[25] How quick is quick? A study done by sales engagement platform company InsideSales in partnership with MIT showed that reps who respond to leads within 5 minutes are 100 times more likely to connect as opposed to those who respond within 30 minutes.[26]

But, according to a study of 433 companies done by conversational marketers at Drift, only 7 percent of companies typically replied to sales leads within five minutes, while 55 percent of companies took five or more days to respond.[27] That's a lot of wasted effort and, potentially, lost sales.

A speedy response can give you a big advantage.

I landed a large deal by using speed as my differentiator. I was in the airport when I got an email that someone had submitted a Contact Me form on our website. I read the complete form on my iPhone and could tell this lead involved some urgency.

I stopped everything, found a corner in the airport, and quickly checked the potential buyer's LinkedIn profile to learn more about his role and company before calling him. He thanked me for responding so quickly, and we spent the next 30 minutes talking about his challenges. We were still talking as I boarded my plane. A few weeks later, I was taking another flight—to meet him in person and discuss a potential solution that could help him address his problems.

When you get in first, you have the chance to collaborate with the customer on the vision and become a strategic partner. It's still essential to sell value, but speed can play a significant part in your wins. That's especially true if your competitors work in a large organization with lots of bureaucracies and bottlenecks.

The moral of the story? Respond as quickly as possible and get an appointment scheduled.

Silence Can Still Help Us Gain Insights

Even if we have world-class prospecting efforts, sometimes our follow-up will be ignored. It's a common experience and an inevitable part of sales.

The first thing to do if your pipeline seems to be drying up is to consider some candid questions:

- Are you using a disciplined approach and prospecting regularly?

- Are you tapping into the full potential of your network?

- Have you gone after the low-hanging fruit?

- Do you have a polished presence online, with a profile that's optimized to get your prospects' attention?

- Are you showing up, adding value, and engaging regularly with prospects on social?

- Are you customizing your outreach communications and using multiple channels (social media, email, phone calls, voicemail messages)?

- Are you providing compelling reasons to meet with you?

- Are you following up quickly and diligently?

It's easy to get into autopilot mode with our prospecting and inadvertently overlook an important step. By answering those questions, you may learn something new or uncover an opportunity to improve your process. Adjust as needed and see how it impacts your response rate.

Sales follow-up is part of a long-term strategy. Sometimes we have to accept that a particular person is not going to agree to meet with us at this time, despite all our efforts. Don't take it personally. But don't burn your bridges or give up on the potential for some sort of relationship with that contact. Things change. People switch jobs. And while it might not happen now, it could later!

ESSENTIAL TAKEAWAYS

- Set aside regular time for prospecting and make it a top priority.

- Build and nurture your network by showing up wherever your prospects are and adding value in every interaction.

- Start your prospecting by going after low-hanging fruit: former customers, referrals, people who said no in the past, people with whom you have shared interests, and companies experiencing compelling events.

- Use multiple channels in your prospecting strategy to increase your response rate.

- Personalize your outbound communications (email, phone calls, voice/video messages) by customizing them and making them relevant to the prospect.

- Have a disciplined follow-up strategy and respond to leads promptly to differentiate yourself.

CHAPTER

7

Prepare for the Discovery Meeting

I'm obsessed with being prepared. Some may call it insecurity; I call it a competitive edge.

It all started when I set foot on the campus of Grandview Elementary School in Hutchinson, Kansas. My family had just immigrated to the United States, and I was in sixth grade. For a while, I felt lost and confused at the new school.

Since English was not my first language, I quickly figured out that I had to work three times harder than other students. Although I fully focused on listening to the teachers or reading the books, I would instantly get thrown offtrack by an unfamiliar word, odd punctuation, or slang phrase I'd never heard of ("what's up?" or "break a leg!").

I discovered an important life lesson that year. Preparation is crucial for survival, whether you're an English as a Second Language (ESL) kid in sixth grade or someone hoping to land a multimillion-dollar enterprise deal.

I also learned that all preparation is not created equal. *More* is not necessarily better. I know because I have personally battled Over-Preparation Syndrome—a term I coined.

There's an opportunity cost associated with spending too much time preparing for a big meeting. (Remember the research rabbit hole?) Eventually there's a point of diminishing returns. I've been there, which is why I stress efficient preparation is more important than just collecting reams of data. Be thorough, but be smart about it.

Here's the good news—preparing *the right amount* for a sales meeting increases your chances of winning deals. An Altify Knowledge Study found that 72 percent of sales participants said account planning increases their understanding of their customers' businesses, and 74 percent of participants cite higher win rates as a key benefit of doing their homework.[1]

In fact, the LinkedIn 2020 State of Sales report found that 56 percent of prospects "strongly agree they're more likely to consider a brand when a sales rep demonstrates a clear understanding of their business needs."[2] I know about that from experience. Preparation is the key to creating a successful discovery meeting.

Scott Collison, president and CEO of community experience platform company Personify, expanded on that idea. "This sounds incredibly basic, but take time to learn about my business," he said. "You don't have to know everything, but if you know the broad strokes of the business, that's an advantage. And if you can come up with some scenarios specific to my business, this leads to a positive meeting. Even if you're not right on the mark, it gives me something to respond to and makes the conversation more engaging."[3]

When talking about preparing for a discovery meeting, I'm referring to "doing your homework"—and that includes some research. While you likely did some research in the prospecting phase to customize your outbound communications, that was at a much higher level than what will be needed for a discovery meeting. It's time for the granular perspective. This research is more specific and provides the detailed background information needed to have a productive, business-level conversation with the prospect.

You've worked hard to get this appointment and want to have every possible chance for success. That means doing what it takes to understand the company, industry, and prospect way beyond a surface level. This chapter prepares you for a meeting that leads to an enterprise sale.

RESEARCH THE BUYER

You may have access to some sophisticated research tools through your company. If so, take advantage of those. Otherwise, you always have alternatives.

Google Them

Never underestimate the free options—including Google. Type the prospect's name into a search engine and look for any social media profiles, news references, or relevant videos.

The prospect's LinkedIn profile is often a great place to start. Identify two things that stand out about this person. How long have they held their current position? Have they worked in other departments or for competitors? Have you attended some of the same business functions? Do you follow the same groups or influencers? How have you helped buyers with similar roles? How does their summary relate to your conversation? Write down those items and bring them up in your sales conversation to begin building the relationship.

Your Google search may also turn up video interviews with your potential buyer. Just by watching a few minutes of a video, you can gain a wide range of insights about the person.

Several years ago, I was selling an enterprise deal. Before I met with the prospect, I found a YouTube video of her presentation at a recent conference. I noticed she emphasized a number of key words aligned to initiatives. When I met with her, I authentically spoke her language—and she noticed.

Starting your research with the person in mind makes the conversation about them, not yourself, which is critical to winning deals and positioning yourself as a partner. Especially in complex deals, developing that connection is vital.

Identify Common Interests for Rapport Building

While researching, look for shared experiences or similar interests that might quickly allow you to build rapport with your prospect on a personal level.

The key is to think of them as a whole person, not just a potential sale. If you can get a sense of who this person is as a human and what he or she cares about, you'll have a natural pathway to building a business relationship.

RESEARCH THE COMPANY

I've been in meetings where a sales rep confidently rattled off industry facts and stats in an effort to impress the potential buyer. Unfortunately, the information had absolutely nothing to do with the prospect or company. Needless to say, the executive was not impressed. For research to add value, it has to be relevant to your buyer's organization.

Complete a More Extensive Online Search

I'll preface this by again saying I realize you did some online research about potential buyers during your prospecting. That's the appetizer; now it's time for the main course. To land larger deals, we have to show up with a hearty level of knowledge so we can speak the prospect's language, focus on their business, and add value. And that requires digging much deeper.

To start, google the company by placing the name in quotation marks (e.g., "ABC Company") and then clicking the News tab. That's a fast way to quickly scan through the headlines and identify a few articles that may resonate with your buyer. You may also uncover information about current projects and initiatives, competitors, and the overall industry that will impact the way you structure your meeting.

The organization's website and LinkedIn page can provide additional information to support your broader Google search, particularly if recent press releases have been posted. If you have access to it, LinkedIn Insights can provide a wealth of valuable data, ranging from the company's headcount growth to quarterly job openings.

These searches can reveal quite a bit about an organization, including any recent trends and compelling events. For example, assume you're selling software that enables customers to instantly monitor and manage their carbon footprints. If your research shows a prospect's company just announced a major commitment to reduce carbon emissions and shift to sustainable resources, you have a natural lead-in to your conversation and an obvious way to align your solutions with their objectives.

Customer review sites also give excellent feedback about how users are responding to the offerings of your prospect's company. You'll get a quick glimpse at the challenges their customers are facing and whether they're happy about the solutions being provided.

In addition to buyer and company information, conduct some basic research on the industry trends. Referencing that information in your discussions showcases your level of interest and knowledge.

Most importantly, be smart and efficient in your search, and always verify the validity of any information uncovered.

As Tom Mendoza, vice chairman at NetApp (formerly president and senior vice president of sales), told me, the buyers' initiatives are not a secret. We just have to know where to look to find them. "I had a guy cold-call me one time," Mendoza explained. "I was in the office and happened to pick up my phone. He said, 'If you give me half an hour, I could solve your three biggest problems.' I said, 'Really, what do you think are my biggest problems?' He answered, 'Well, that's why I need to meet with you.' I replied, 'Let me help you. I'm not secretive about my problems. Why don't you go find out what they are, and if you can solve them, I'll meet with you.'"[4]

To set yourself up for success in a discovery meeting, efficient research and preparation are mandatory.

Scan Earnings Call Transcripts

When getting ready for discovery calls with public companies, I habitually check their earnings call transcripts. These are transcribed versions of leadership announcements about the company's financials for the quarter. They are free and can be found by simply googling them. It's a fast way to glean the most current information about the organization's fiscal health.

To be efficient, search for words relevant to your solution and to your buyer's persona using your computer's Find function. (For MS Windows OS, press and hold Ctrl-F. For Mac, press Command + F.) Then incorporate this information in your discovery meeting to validate your understanding of your prospect's needs, collaborate with them, and customize the conversation around their business. Throughout my career, this technique has helped me uncover opportunities with my prospects and position my solutions as strategic to their business outcomes.

I've also unearthed some great information in the question-and-answer (Q&A) section at the end of the transcripts. This part features questions analysts ask the leaders at the close of the call, and they can be quite pointed. Sometimes analysts ask about specific challenges the company is facing or bring up topics that may not have been discussed in depth. If the analysts express concern about certain areas, you better believe the leaders want to calm those fears. So, if you have a solution for those business challenges, your meeting can be timely and well received.

When you use information from earnings call transcripts, be sure to let your prospects know that. It shows them you tried to understand their organizations on a deeper level. You're demonstrating you are focused on their businesses, not simply on your product's features and functions.

For example, let's say you're preparing to meet with the executive vice president (EVP) of a public company. In the earnings call transcript, the CEO talked about the tremendous growth in that EVP's business unit. The CEO also mentioned the company was hiring lots of new salespeople, domestically and internationally.

Imagine bringing that targeted information up in your conversation with the EVP, followed by a relevant question unpacking the company's initiatives. That could open the door for you to share insights and uncover potential opportunities to add value.

That might sound like this:

> As I was preparing for this appointment, I checked your Q2 earnings call transcript. Your CEO discussed the growth in your BU and the number of new hires you recruited in the last quarter. Congratulations! I'm curious . . . how are you streamlining your onboarding process?

Integrating this research makes the conversation more strategic, allowing you to focus on your potential buyer's business and the priorities they have established. It also creates a space to discuss initiatives, insights, trends, and stories.

CONNECT THE DOTS

Once your research is complete, analyze the information you've gathered and start pulling everything together:

- Develop questions you might ask during your discovery meeting, but be ready to actively listen so you can adapt them based on the information shared by your prospects.
- Identify potential customer stories that might resonate with your prospects.
- Be ready to share insights that someone with this buyer persona would typically find of value.

Keep in mind that these should not be the garden-variety kind of questions that could be answered with a Google search. These questions should be thoughtfully strategic and remain focused on the prospect's business outcomes. Connect the dots! For example:

- What stood out most about the buyer or the company? Is there a compelling event? New leadership? An organizational restructure? Some type of transformation?

- What did you discover about the industry or competitors that intrigued you? Any insights? Trends?

- Did you notice anything missing or confusing in the research?

- How can you structure your questions to show that your top priority is helping potential customers achieve their goals?

By walking into a discovery meeting prepared—armed with the right amount of research, strategic questions, and valuable insights with a customer-centric perspective—you're positioning yourself as a strategic partner rather than a commodity. Even better, you'll have the

3 Steps to Prepare for a Discovery Meeting

1. Research the Buyer
   - Google them
   - Identify common interests for rapport building

2. Research the Company
   - Complete a more extensive online search
   - Scan earnings call transcripts for public companies

3. Connect the Dots

tools to elevate the quality of your conversations, proposals, and, ultimately, relationships.

Checklists for discovery meeting preparation and best practices, as well as a blank **Discovery Meeting Organizer**, are available in the **Sales Essentials Toolkit** at the end of the book.

ESSENTIAL TAKEAWAYS

- Research the buyer by googling them and looking for any social media profiles, news references, or relevant videos.

- Familiarize yourself with your buyer's LinkedIn profile and identify information relevant to the meeting, as well as shared experiences to build rapport.

- Google the company, scanning for headlines, current projects, initiatives, and overall industry information.

- Check out the company's website and LinkedIn page for additional information such as recent press releases.

- Scan earnings call transcripts for public companies and use your findings to personalize your conversations.

- Organize your research to help you develop relevant questions, identify insights to share, and determine potential customer stories that can add value for the prospect.

INTERACTIVE EXERCISE 1

BEFORE THE SALE

Read the case study and use the information you learned in this section to answer the strategy questions that follow. (An Exercise Answer Key can be found at the end of the book.)

Lydia works in sales for a company that develops backup/recovery software and cybersecurity solutions for a variety of industries. She launched a prospecting campaign several months ago, targeting one of her buyer personas: chief information officers (CIOs) for large banks. Lydia's efforts included a variety of customized LinkedIn posts that led to some engagement with Roger, the CIO for a prominent group of banks located on the East Coast.

After reaching out with multiple emails, calls, and voicemail messages, it finally happened. Lydia got an email response from Roger expressing interest in meeting with her. She quickly replied and was thrilled to schedule a discovery meeting.

In preparing for the meeting, Lydia took these actions:

- She googled the bank and checked the News section. She found out a recent data breach exposed sensitive details about two million customers and resulted in unspecified data loss. The company was struggling with the public relations backlash, and its stock prices had tumbled 14 percent.

- She checked the organization's most recent earnings call transcript. The CEO enthusiastically discussed the company's growth strategy, specifically the pending acquisition of a smaller chain of banks in Boston with the potential to increase revenue by 20 percent over five years. Lydia noticed in the Q&A section that analysts were pushing the CEO to talk more about the data breach, the status of the company's digital transformation, and plans for IT systems to support corporate growth in a secure and reliable way.

- She googled Roger and looked to see if he appeared in the News section. She found an article about his recent presentation at a financial industry conference; it described in detail his philosophy about maintaining the integrity of the bank's IT systems. That gave her an excellent picture of his priorities and areas of emphasis. She also saw that his most recent activities on LinkedIn included liking and commenting on an article about data backup being the key to digital transformation.

- In Roger's LinkedIn profile, she noticed a shared connection—Darnell, a former colleague. She contacted Darnell and got some valuable insight about Roger. He was an analytical thinker, highly organized, direct but open-minded with a dry sense of humor, and very athletic.

- Scanning Roger's LinkedIn posts for the past few years, she discovered he was an avid skydiver. Lydia had recently made her first jump, with another one scheduled in six weeks.

STRATEGY QUESTIONS

1. How can Lydia build rapport with Roger to pave the way for a professional relationship?

2. How can Lydia incorporate her research from Google and LinkedIn to improve the quality of the discovery meeting?

3. How can Lydia leverage the information about Roger shared by Darnell to make a greater impact?

CHAPTER

8

Make a Positive
First Impression

To summarize this chapter: How we show up *really* matters. But, there's much more that goes into this than you might imagine, so keep reading.

From experience, I know showing up matters, so it's something I consistently highlight when training others.

I remember landing an important sales meeting with what had the potential to be a major customer. I worked like crazy to get this appointment and was understandably excited. I bought a new suit and rewarded myself with some pink Chanel lip gloss. I was dressed and ready to go.

Arriving 30 minutes early, my colleague and I signed in and waited in the lobby. She leaned in and quietly said. "Rana, you've got this! I just have one suggestion." I paused and took a deep breath. "OK, what is it?" I asked.

"I think you have on too much lip gloss. It's distracting."

While I was a little embarrassed, I also appreciated her candor and knew she had good intentions. I went into the restroom and looked in the mirror. Yep, she was right! I was proud I could finally afford some Chanel cosmetics, but I had to remind myself: I'm *not* selling lip gloss.

LEVERAGING NONVERBAL COMMUNICATION

Experiments conducted by Princeton University psychologists Janine Wills and Alexander Todorov found that it takes a tenth of a second for someone to form a first impression of a person they just met on traits such as attractiveness, likeability, competence, trustworthiness, and aggressiveness. One-tenth of one second![1]

Before we ever say a word, our nonverbal communication speaks volumes about us. People automatically make snap judgments about our personalities and credibility based on our facial expressions, body language, attire, and demeanor. And once we do open our mouths, people hear more than just our words.

Let's look at some components of nonverbal communication that make up first impressions during a discovery meeting.

Attire and Accessories

Several studies have shown that clothing plays a role in forming first impressions.[2] For the record, I'm referring not only to the suits, pants, or dresses we choose to wear as salespeople. First-impression-makers also extend to our shoes, briefcases, jewelry, eyeglasses, hairstyles, and makeup.

If we want to convince a prospect to trust us with a multimillion-dollar enterprise deal, we need to project visual credibility. That doesn't mean we have to spend $5,000 on a custom-made outfit. But it definitely sends a message to our prospects if we arrive at the discovery meeting with clothes that are wrinkled, ill-fitting, or hopelessly out of season.

The thought running through the potential buyer's head might be: *Meeting with me clearly wasn't a priority. If my account will get the same level of attention as this sales rep's attire, we can end this now and save us both a lot of time.*

The rule of thumb is to dress appropriately based on the audience, setting, and purpose of the meeting, as well as the organization's culture.

I once had a discovery meeting with a growing organization. I did my homework and was ready to impress. I put on my signature black suit and black heels. But the minute I walked into the lobby, I realized something didn't feel right. The atmosphere in the office was distinctly laid-back—open spaces, creative artwork on the walls, casually dressed employees, and lots of energy and laughter.

I looked totally out of place in my serious business attire and felt like a nerd in high school among all the cool kids. That feeling was even more pronounced when I met with the key decision maker. He was dressed neatly but casually and had a very relaxed demeanor. Meanwhile, I was prepared to give a formal presentation in my uptight suit. That poor guy! He probably felt like he was back in college, forced to listen to a lecture.

The disconnect was obvious, and the whole thing was uncomfortable. And, in case you were wondering, there were definitely no follow-up meetings.

Because attire influences first impressions, make sure to visually demonstrate you want to earn the business. That means adapting to their environment and level of formality while still remaining authentically you. I'm not suggesting choosing attire that's out of character just to fit in, but make an effort within reason. Remember, the visual package you present will impact the way you are perceived and the way your presentation is interpreted. Make it count!

Sometimes you simply have no way of knowing what type of environment you'll encounter at a prospect's place of business, which is complicated because there's such a wide range of office dress codes these days. In those situations, I err on the side of caution and go with business casual attire. Not too formal, but not too laid-back. I won't stick out if it's casual Friday, and I'll fit in if everyone is wearing suits.

It's important to demonstrate you care about being "on target" with your appearance as much as you do your presentation. Establishing that visual parity reinforces the message that you want to partner with them.

Facial Expressions

Another element of nonverbal communication that plays into first impressions is the message sent by our facial expressions.

For example, when meeting your prospect for the first time, do you make natural eye contact and present an authentic smile? Researchers found that *Duchenne smiles* increase the credibility of our words.[3] These are genuine smiles that raise your cheeks and reach your eyes, causing them to narrow slightly.

Another research study published in SAGE journals found that happy facial expressions increase trustworthiness ratings. For example, in one study, participants noted that they were more likely to vote for candidates that exhibited happy expressions and also more likely to loan them money. The conclusion? Even subtly happy expressions can impact others' behaviors.[4]

If you can use your facial expressions to improve your first impression with a potential buyer, you'll make a valuable connection that serves you well during the meeting.

Body Language

It's no surprise that nonverbal communication relayed by our body language impacts how people perceive us and our messages. In fact, some researchers have noted people tend to give more weight to nonverbal messages when there's a misalignment between someone's verbal and nonverbal communication.

For example, one study showed that a mismatch was perceived as an expression of irony.[5] Another study found that subjects who presented messages with "gesture-speech mismatches" were considered less likable and less believable by participants.[6]

For these reasons, it's critical to be aware of our body language and the impact it has on the first impressions we form. In fact, research shows that our posture impacts the way we're perceived, particularly when it comes to what scientists refer to as *expansive or contractive postures*.[7] Generally speaking, people who fully stand up and occupy more space are seen as confident and powerful. Those who hunch over with their arms crossed or hands folded seem nervous, closed-off, or unapproachable.

The recommendations? Think about the body language you use and the image you're projecting when first meeting your prospects:

- Do you stand tall with an open stance when greeting them for the first time?

- Do you lean in slightly to shake hands?

- Do you sit up with your back straight or slump down in the chair?

- Do you nod gently as they speak?

- Do you use natural, appropriate hand gestures?

To make a positive first impression with our body language, we have to work at authentically integrating these habits.

When I originally got into sales, I felt anxious and insecure about meeting prospects face-to-face. While I was well prepared and could answer their questions, the early outcomes were not positive. I would get so irritated—especially when others were sharing the same information and gaining traction. I knew I was using the right words, bringing in solid research, and sharing pertinent data. And yet, there was very little positive response.

I started asking for candid feedback from other colleagues who attended meetings with me. Their paraphrased comments certainly shed some light on the situation:

> "I think it would help if you made more eye contact."

> "You kind of looked like a deer in the headlights in that meeting."

> "I know you were really focused (and maybe a little nervous), but it seemed like you were just frozen in your chair during the whole appointment."

Mystery solved. My body language was undermining my knowledge and expertise. My nonverbal communication wasn't aligned with my words. While the deer-in-the-headlight look might have gained me some sympathy, it never won me a deal!

Since then, I've spent many weekends recording myself making presentations, trying to get alignment between what I was saying and what clients would be seeing. I had to continuously practice making eye contact with the camera and loosening up to incorporate natural movement into my interactions. The more recordings I made, the more I realized how much my nonverbal communication had been holding me back.

If you haven't recorded yourself practicing your sales pitch, I encourage you to include that as a regular part of your preparation. Be brutally honest: What is your body language saying to your customers? Not knowing the answer to that could be a major barrier to your success. Uncover the problems and make the adjustments that will support your ability to sell at the highest level.

Attitude

As leadership expert and author John Maxwell said, "People may not hear your words, but they feel your attitude."[8] The point? We're communicating even when we aren't speaking. In fact, studies have shown that our demeanor and attitudes influence our performance,[9] as well as our customers' impressions of us.

Scientists from Stanford University used MRI scans to map the neurological effects of having a positive attitude, and they found a direct link to achievement.[10] That impact was echoed in *Mindset: The New Psychology of Success* by Stanford professor Carol Dweck. She discovered that people with a growth mindset—the belief that they could develop their abilities and make improvements—outperform those with a fixed mindset, even if their IQs are lower.[11]

Even if we have the best of intentions to maintain a positive attitude, many of us are juggling back-to-back meetings with endless to-do lists racing through our heads. We're overwhelmed and rushed.

Prospects pick up on that, loud and clear. And it's contagious! Just remember that a positive attitude invites positive outcomes—and vice versa. If you go into a meeting looking defeated and believing there's no way you'll ever land the deal, you'll be absolutely correct.

Adjusting your attitude transforms your potential for success. Take a little time before a discovery meeting to clear out the mental clutter from the day and think about the possibilities for a long, profitable relationship with this potential buyer. It's powerful!

In your meetings, show your future customers they are the most important thing in your mind at this exact moment. According to Salesforce's State of the Connected Customer report (second edition), 84 percent of B2B buyers said that "being treated like a person, not a number, is very important to winning their business."[12] We can project that attitude through our nonverbal communication. A different demeanor can create a different outcome.

Tone of Voice

Admittedly, this one blurs the line between verbal and nonverbal communications, but it's an aspect that goes beyond just the words we say to a prospect. Our voices are actually powerful tools that play a major role in the impression we leave on potential buyers. We touched on this briefly when discussing prospecting calls, but this is where it really becomes a pivotal component.

Here are a few aspects to keep in mind about your tone of voice in a discovery meeting:

- **Pitch.** In one study, researchers recorded men and women saying, "I urge you to vote for me this November."[13] They modified each of the original voices to yield versions that were slightly higher and lower. Then they asked participants to vote for these "candidates" based only on their voices. The results? People consistently chose the candidates with lower-pitched voices, regardless of the gender.[14] Some studies have also linked pitch of our voices with perceptions about our competence and trustworthiness.[15]

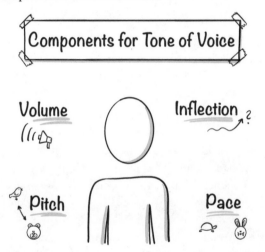

This isn't about trying to sound like someone you're not, being deceptive or inauthentic. It's more about finding a balance and adjusting accordingly. Practice speaking in the lower register of your voice. Then, when you want to come across as more credible and confident, be intentional about lowering your pitch.

- **Pace.** How fast or slow do you typically speak? Recording yourself rehearsing your presentations is very helpful here, as well. If you're chattering at top speed, you may sound nervous or overcaffeinated. However, speaking too slowly and deliberately may lose the potential buyer's attention and even create some frustration.

A good option, in general, is to follow the prospect's pace. Balance is always the key. This is particularly important when you have a thick accent or if English is your second language. If you speak too quickly, your audience will be lost.

- **Volume.** Again, matching the loudness of the prospect's speech is always a safe bet. Your speech volume says a lot about your energy and confidence levels. Up to a point, of course.

- **Inflection.** Do you use a natural tone that's appropriate for different parts of your sentences? A common challenge here is *upspeak*. That's when we're saying a sentence that ends with a period, but our inflection rises at the end as though it were a question. It confuses the listeners and makes us sound unsure about the statement. If we do it habitually, it undercuts our credibility.

  I was in a meeting where the person running it started allowing upspeak to creep into his voice multiple times. One stakeholder finally interrupted: "So, are you telling us something or asking a question?"

  To reduce upspeak, get feedback from trusted colleagues about your conversation style. And then practice, practice, practice. Hold yourself accountable.

  Another facet of inflection is the way we emphasize key words, which tells listeners what is important and helps them interpret our messages. The challenge here? The meaning of a sentence can be changed simply by changing the emphasis. Getting it wrong in a discovery meeting may be a huge liability. But when our emphasis is spot-on, it helps us influence our prospects and increase their understanding of our solutions.

Overall, our voices communicate a wealth of information about us to our prospects. And while there are physiological limitations on how many changes we can make to our voices, we need to be aware of the impact and adjust accordingly.

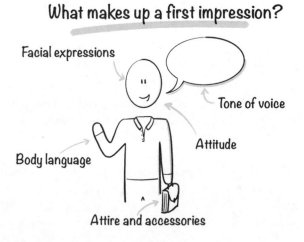

What makes up a first impression?

Facial expressions

Tone of voice

Attitude

Body language

Attire and accessories

POSITIONING YOURSELF AS A PARTNER

The other side of the coin in terms of "how we show up" for a discovery meeting involves setting the stage for our role in the relationship. Think about how our words and actions in the first few minutes of a meeting can influence the way potential buyers perceive us.

As part of making a first impression, our initial statements and comments signal to our prospects whether we are:

- At a junior level
- Just trying to make a sale
- More concerned with meeting quota than helping the customer solve a problem

  Versus . . .

- A credible and knowledgeable peer
- A trusted consultant and advisor
- A partner in building the customer's business

The impact is vastly different. That's why it's critical to be aware of how we represent ourselves to our buyers and consciously work toward being perceived as partners in their success. This process starts from the first contact with a prospect and continues through the discovery meeting, the sale, and beyond.

By positioning ourselves as partners, we display more than knowledge and competence. It's about character and trust. We show our willingness to do the right thing for a customer, even if it means losing a sale. We put their interests above ours and deliver on promises.

There are some specific things you can do to set yourself up as a partner in these initial sales discussions.

Show You're Prepared

Know the goal of the meeting, and be proactive about exploring the challenges that need to be addressed. We've talked extensively about things you can do to be prepared for discovery meetings. Once you're there, make sure your conversations lead with the customer and add value while selectively showcasing your preparation. That's an outstanding way to set yourself up as a committed and engaged partner in the process.

Demonstrate Good Intentions up Front

Express your interest in discovering whether your offerings are the right solution for the customer—or if something else is a better fit. Sounds counterproductive, but it builds trust and shows you care about *their* success.

These initial sales conversations are critical for you and the prospect to determine if this partnership is a good fit. By focusing on the best choices for them, you'll build stronger relationships. While it might not work out now, this honesty and integrity won't go unnoticed. I've sometimes walked away from deals because the fit wasn't right, only to have the prospect refer me to a colleague. In other situations, the "lost" prospect became a customer at a later time.

Simplify the Process

Many customers are overwhelmed by the sheer volume of information that comes their way on a daily basis. By being sensitive to that and trying to make things easier for them, we reinforce our role as a partner.

According to a *Harvard Business Review* article, the top sales reps "emphasize simplicity over comprehensiveness. . . . They help customers make sense of the information they've encountered."[16] They explain things in simple terms and don't flood the prospect with unnecessary messages. They also objectively provide all the information (pros and cons) and give prospects the space to feel confident about making the best decisions for their businesses.

The authors of the article cited some interesting statistics, including that 80 percent of buyers who engaged with "sensemaking" reps reported completing high-quality, low-regret purchases. That number dropped to 50 percent when reps just verbally told them all the information and 30 percent when reps gave them the facts to read on their own.[17]

Make an Impact Early

To be a true consultant, we need to add value for our prospects throughout the entire sales process and beyond, but it's particularly important as part of making a positive first impression. If we don't make an impact early, there might not be a second chance.

Be proactive about finding opportunities to share insights with prospects from the first meeting. This may include information gained through unique experiences working with similar customers, attending trade shows, or participating in business events. Sometimes the patterns, themes, and trends we detect from our vantage point can be extremely valuable for them, so don't underestimate it.

The same goes for alerting prospects to red flags we're seeing in the industry. Sometimes we add value by sharing advice our customers don't necessarily want to hear. While challenging the prospect's thinking might feel uncomfortable, it could actually pay off if done in a tactful, value-added way with the positive intention of helping them achieve their goals.

According to LinkedIn's 2022 Global State of Sales report, 89 percent of buyers surveyed said they want their reps to challenge them.

In other words, differentiate yourself by challenging the status quo and asking questions that lead your customers to think in different ways.[18]

That knowledge can set you apart. According to Salesforce's State of Sales report (third edition), 78 percent of business buyers are looking for trusted advisors—not just salespeople—who can add value to their businesses.[19]

Be Transparent

An excellent way to build trust as a partner in your discovery meetings is to have transparency in your conversations.

If you don't know something, don't try to fake your way through an answer. Your buyers will feel it. Remember there's power in the honesty of being human. Customers don't expect reps to know absolutely everything, so it's perfectly acceptable to say: "That's a great question! I don't really know the answer, but I'll find out and get back to you this week." Write it down and make sure to keep your word.

The first impressions we form at the start of our discovery meetings set the tone for everything that follows. By displaying visual credibility and positioning ourselves as trusted advisors, we accelerate trust-building and move our conversations more quickly to a strategic level.

A checklist for managing your first impressions is available in the Sales Essentials Toolkit at the end of the book.

ESSENTIAL TAKEAWAYS

- Dress appropriately for discovery meetings based on the audience, setting, and purpose of the meeting, as well as the organization's culture.

- Use facial expressions to improve the first impression you make on a potential buyer.

- Ensure alignment between your verbal and nonverbal communications.

- Take steps to make sure your body language is creating the image you want to portray.

- Be mentally present and project a positive attitude.

- Pay attention to your tone of voice, including pitch, pace, volume, and inflection.

- Consciously work to present yourself to prospects as a partner in their success.

CHAPTER
9

Manage the Discovery Meeting

Your preparation is complete. First impressions have been made and now it's showtime! The goal for your discovery meeting is to quickly qualify in ("Yes, this prospect makes good sense as a potential buyer") or qualify out ("We currently don't have the right solution for this customer").

There are nine steps that lead to a successful discovery meeting.

STEP 1: MAKE INTRODUCTIONS

Whether your discovery meeting includes two people or an entire group, start with introductions.

You've probably been in a situation when the person running the meeting said, "OK, we're all here. Let's get started!" Meanwhile, you're wondering: *Who's "we"?* This is particularly common in a virtual setting. Take a moment to determine exactly who's participating in the conversation.

If additional people from *your* organization are participating in the meeting, introduce them to the potential buyer with their names and titles. Every team member should also be prepared to share a brief overview of their role so the prospect isn't wondering why they are part of the conversation.

As you move through the introduction process, validate any facts you gathered as a conversation-starter:

> I understand from your LinkedIn profile that you are in a new role as VP of sales and, before that, you were a sales representative. I'm looking forward to learning more about how your experience in the field shapes your current vision.

If your research didn't turn up any clues about how to pronounce someone's name, be sure to ask. I make that part of my process and then use their name throughout the conversation (without overdoing it, of course).

STEP 2: BUILD RAPPORT

I know you're thinking: *Yeah, yeah, yeah. Build rapport. Duh. I get it.* Before you skip ahead, here's a statistic that may change your mind. In a study by Gong, sales reps selling enterprise deals who spent more time on rapport-building conversations had a higher closing ratio.[1] It's not an exercise that you should consider optional or automatic. It's required and intentional.

So what is rapport exactly? Rapport is a genuine connection you make with another person. It happens when you find things you have in common. It's an authentic emotional bond that forms when two people come together over a shared topic.

Remember those common interests and connections you uncovered during the research phase? This is the time to integrate them into your conversations.

I remember scheduling a first meeting with an executive and feeling a little intimidated. I started to wonder if we would have any similarities at all. However, in my research, I discovered he was a runner. In the first few minutes of the discovery meeting, I brought that up and told him I was also a runner. We took time to share our experiences, and he told me he was preparing for a marathon. That conversation warmed everything up! It also reframed the meeting as a business discussion between two people who shared the same interest.

In another instance, I saw that my prospect was originally from a town in Kansas—not far from where my family immigrated. That Midwest connection was special, and we spent a few minutes talking about the experience. The memories were funny and charming. Again, the tone was set.

So, what if you can't find anything you have in common with the prospect besides being a living, breathing human? It happens. In those cases, find something about them that genuinely interests you and start a conversation about that topic. For example:

> "I noticed you posted something about climbing Mount Kilimanjaro a couple of years ago. I can imagine that took a lot of preparation. I'm curious, how did you train for it?"

> "I read that you volunteer for Habitat for Humanity. I've always wanted to do that, but I'm unsure about the time commitment. How did you manage that?"

Before wrapping up this topic, I feel the need to add a word of caution.

While building rapport is an essential part of connecting before you move on to business, it shouldn't take a long time. First of all, you have a goal to accomplish. Spending too much time on building rapport cuts into the time needed to achieve your objectives. In addition, some buyers don't have the patience for too much of that. They are extremely busy or singularly focused on reaching their goals. Read their nonverbal communication cues to know when it's time to move on. Finding the right balance will tee up a great business conversation.

STEP 3: AGREE ON THE AGENDA

We know the importance of having an agenda to guide a meeting. That helps to avoid the awkward moment, 15 minutes in, when someone says, "Remind me again, what are we trying to accomplish today?"

Make it a habit to identify three areas you want to discuss in a meeting and share them with the participants in advance. Include those items in the calendar invitation and revisit them at the start of the meeting to confirm that everyone agrees—or adjust accordingly. When you give attendees an opportunity to play a part in forming the agenda, there's a higher chance they will show up, pay attention, and participate. That's because they understand the goal of the meeting and see value in the conversation.

Getting buy-in on the agenda is particularly important when people have hectic schedules and competing priorities. According to Harvard Business School, professionals attended 12.9 percent more meetings during the Covid-19 pandemic, and the number of people invited to each meeting increased by 13.5 percent.[2]

Why am I sharing that? Because we are all getting inundated with calendar invitations to attend meetings, and we often have to make some choices. Develop an agenda that makes clear to the participants why this conversation will be meaningful for them.

STEP 4: CONDUCT A BUSINESS-LEVEL CONVERSATION

With the agenda confirmed, shift your discovery meeting into the main event: engaging in a business-level conversation.

That means focusing on the prospect's business with little or no discussion about your products and solutions. At least not yet. The idea is to uncover information about the potential customer's initiatives, goals, and challenges in a sophisticated way that shows we have done our homework. Once we have that information, we are better prepared to share relevant stories and add value with related insights.

Asking the right questions can be a real game changer during a discovery meeting. More specifically, those questions play a dual role. First of all, they help gather the information we need to uncover opportunities and create customized solutions with differentiators that are important to the customer. Furthermore, they build our credibility and help us validate and understand the customers' needs.

Research published in the *Journal of Personality and Social Psychology* found a strong relationship between asking questions and being seen as likable. People who asked more questions (specifically follow-up questions) were perceived more favorably by their conversation partners.[3]

Despite that advantage, current research also shows that most of us don't ask enough questions during meetings. One explanation for that? Some people simply don't understand the benefits of asking questions.[4] Other reasons cited follow some similar themes, such as not wanting to sound incompetent or rude.[5] Don't let those fears prevent you from participating in a robust, two-way dialogue with prospects that demonstrates your interest and showcases your knowledge.

It's worth noting that questions in business-level conversations should be strategic and intentional rather than generic. Here are two examples to illustrate the difference:

Basic Questions	Business-Level Questions
Do you have supply chain challenges?	I saw an interview with your CEO, and he mentioned the challenges your company is facing with the supply chain crisis. How much impact will this have on your revenue this year?
Can you tell me about your onboarding program?	I read in your most recent earnings call transcript that your total revenue for Q1 2022 was $600 million, up 25 percent year over year. Your sales force also grew by 88 percent in the last year. I'm curious to hear about your onboarding program. . . .

STEP 5: LISTEN ACTIVELY

All of the good questions in the world can't help land a deal if we don't pay close attention to the responses. In fact, active listening might be one of the most important things in our sales toolkit. It also is one of the toughest things to do, considering that many of us in sales have competitive personalities and deadline-oriented thinking. Self-restraint is often in short supply.

However, today's top sales reps do seem to be talking less, according to studies by Chorus and Gong.[6,7] For example, Gong analyzed the optimal talking-to-listening ratio during sales calls. The highest conversion rate on B2B conversations was approximately 43 percent talking and 57 percent listening.[8]

The lesson? If we're doing more talking than listening during discovery meetings, we're doing it wrong.

Here are some best practices to help you become a better listener.

Be Present

Set your phone to silent mode and put it away. If you're conducting a virtual meeting, close your email and turn off notifications. Eliminate distractions, and don't give in to the temptation to multitask!

Use Nonverbal Cues to Acknowledge You're Listening

Make natural eye contact and, when appropriate, use a slight nod, head tilt, or smile to indicate you're following their explanations.

Pay Attention to Body Language and Facial Expressions

How are prospects feeling about the conversation? What are they *not* saying? Can you detect a topic that makes them uncomfortable? Read between the lines.

Listen for Names of Key Players

If potential buyers mention decision makers or influencers, ask for more information about them, as well as their job functions and roles. Request an introduction if they are part of the sales process. At a minimum, jot down their names so you can later research their backgrounds and determine their level of influence. Remember, your prospects mentioned them for a reason. Find out what that is, so you don't get blindsided later.

Ask Intelligent Follow-up Questions

Your choice of questions after the prospect speaks can demonstrate that you are genuinely listening, not just running down a list of canned questions. According to *Harvard Business Review*, asking good follow-up questions can have an extraordinary impact on a conversation.[9] It demonstrates that you heard them, you care, and you want to learn more about their topic. This is also an excellent way to take discussions to a deeper level.

Strong follow-up questions that demonstrate true listening include:

- Clarifying a comment made

- Asking for confirmation about a particular point

- Summarizing or paraphrasing their key messages

- Reflecting, validating, or showing empathy on a certain subject

Practice the Intentional Pause

Even if we exhibit world-class listening skills, we may reduce our effectiveness by jumping in too quickly to speak after the prospect stops talking. A few seconds of silence is actually good. It creates space for people to think and even invites the potential buyer to add on another nugget of information that just might be exactly what we need to hear.

Record the Meeting

If you regularly conduct virtual discovery meetings or phone calls, you may already have the tools available to record your sales conversations. But if not, put the pieces in place to make that possible. Be sure to consistently follow the correct protocol by always informing those on the call that you're taping the discussion.

Recording yourself is the best way to assess your listening performance, increase your self-awareness, and identify room for improvement. Did you talk more than listen? Did you miss any opportunities for great follow-up questions?

STEP 6: BE STRATEGIC ABOUT VISUALS

Appropriate visuals used during meetings can be quite effective, but I'm not endorsing "Death by PowerPoint" with dozens of slides showing features and function tables.

The visuals in a discovery meeting focus on the customer, again using an outside-in perspective. Accomplish this by incorporating relevant, compelling graphics that cut through the clutter and sustain your prospect's attention.

Keep in mind that every visual aid doesn't translate into an automatic advantage. These tools are only powerful if they are pertinent, concise, and easy to understand. Be strategic about the visuals selected to support your message; don't let them create a barrier between you and your prospects.

What does that mean? Especially in a virtual environment, it can be tempting to screen-share throughout the whole meeting. I've found that mixing channels is a better solution to keep the prospects engaged. For example, present a few slides but then stop the screen-share and return to a face-to-face discussion between you and the potential buyer. That keeps the personal conversation as the centerpiece of the meeting.

STEP 7: QUALIFY THE OPPORTUNITY

I'm an eternal optimist and always hope for positive outcomes. But experience quickly taught me hope is not a strategy. To succeed on a larger scale, I had to make sure I was spending my time in the right places with the right deals—and walking away from those that weren't a good fit.

An executive I once interviewed, Ganesh Padmanabhan, explained the irony and quoted one of his mentors: "There are two winners in a deal. Those who get the contract, and those who get out first."[10]

For every minute spent on the *wrong* deal, we could be spending time to land one that's right: a multimillion-dollar customer with excellent potential for growth and expansion.

The opportunity cost is significant! It's a concept I didn't fully understand early on, but I eventually gained the discipline to be comfortable walking away when the partnership isn't a great fit for both parties.

One of my experiences on the way to that epiphany involved landing a small deal with a customer that wasn't part of my buyer profile. I recognized the disconnect but couldn't resist the lure of making another sale. After pushing hard to get the contract, I had to put an inordinate amount of pressure on myself and my team to deliver. The customer's needs didn't match up with the usual solutions we offered, requiring a disproportionate amount of my time. It also took resources away from other areas ripe with opportunities. We ended up delivering, but definitely at a cost.

As part of discovery meetings, always make sure you are qualifying the opportunity. Even if you can convince the prospect to say yes, objectively analyze whether this is truly a good partnership:

- Based on your discovery conversation, does the prospect's organization match your buyer profile?

- Based on your discovery conversation, does the prospect match your buyer persona?

- Does your product/solution solve a business problem for this customer?

- Does the prospect see the value in what you are offering?

- What is the timeline for the prospect to achieve the pertinent objectives?

- Can you deliver on the prospect's objectives within the specified time frame?

- Do you detect signs of interest in buying? *(responding to your emails, inviting others to the meeting, etc.)*

- What is the role of the prospect in making a final decision? *(coach, champion, budget holder, etc.)*

- Do you know the decision-making process inside the company and the roles of additional people you're meeting?

- Does the company have the budget available? Or can they reallocate funds to be able to afford your solution?

- Is there a compelling event that increases the sense of urgency for purchasing your solution? *(data breach, recent competitive product launch, new compliance regulations, etc.)*

A complete checklist of best practices to help you qualify your prospects is available in the Sales Essentials Toolkit at the end of the book.

While you won't officially discuss pricing with the prospect until you present your proposal, it's also important to make sure this potential project is at least in the general realm of possibility. Often it is helpful to provide a range of pricing in the discovery meeting to see what kind of reaction that generates. If there's an obvious disconnect, move on. It is better to qualify the deal out before investing a huge amount of time to create a complex, customized proposal.

If you are new to sales or to a particular industry, ask your manager if there are other pertinent questions that may be crucial parts of the discovery process.

Qualifying an opportunity should also be viewed as an ongoing task. On one occasion, I remember moving a deal into the proposal stage, only to find out that I wasn't talking to the right person. I also couldn't clearly articulate the company's challenges and drivers, which was a big red flag. The time I wasted on that deal is a reminder of the importance of following some proven guidelines: understand the internal decision-making process early on, be clear about the role of the contact person, and get in front of the right people sooner rather than later.

STEP 8: CONFIRM NEXT STEPS

I still remember my excitement after a discovery call went particularly well. And then my manager casually asked, "So, what are the next steps?" My celebration immediately turned into an "Oh crap!" moment. I had no idea. I invested all that time up front, meticulously preparing to get the discovery meeting, but had no plan to move things forward.

As I matured in my career (and paid the price for several hiccups), I started being very intentional about establishing next steps with my prospects. In fact, years ago, I made it a habit to include that in my agenda and put a big sticky note on my computer as a reminder to make time for next steps during virtual meetings. I even establish the expectations from the beginning: "At the end of this conversation, we'll both decide what the appropriate next steps are."

So, what's the best way to approach "what happens next" in the discovery meeting?

- Be deliberate about allowing time in the meeting to define next steps.

- Summarize the discussion before establishing the follow-up plan.

- Collaborate with the prospect and ask for input in determining next steps.

- Select a date and time for another meeting if appropriate.

STEP 9: PROMPTLY TAKE ACTION

After leaving a discovery meeting, there are several things that need to be done right away:

- Send a calendar invitation to confirm the next appointment.

- Craft a personalized email with an overview of the discovery meeting conversation and reiterate next steps.

- Forward any information you promised to send them (i.e., a white paper, research study, pertinent article).

- Reach out to any people you agreed to contact.

The way we respond after an initial appointment helps establish trust with potential buyers. Not following through promptly sends an unflattering message about our reliability and willingness to keep promises.

There's one other tip I'd like to share regarding following up. If you just met the prospect for the first time during the discovery meeting, take a moment to send a handwritten note of thanks. I mentioned this in Chapter 6, and I do think it's a viable outreach channel that deserves attention.

Global brand consulting firm Millward Brown (now the Kantar Group) teamed up with the Centre for Experimental Consumer Psychology to study how the human brain processes physical materials (such as notes and letters) compared with digital materials (such as emails and social media messages).[11]

They found that physical materials seem more tangible and real to our brains, which leads us to process them on a more emotional level.[12] So following up with a prospect with a handwritten note creates a more memorable and relatable impression. Be sure to mention something that authentically resonated with you in the meeting and personalize it so that it means something to you and your prospect.

Now, I'm not suggesting that jotting down a quick handwritten note is going to land the sale. However, it is a way to differentiate yourself from your competition, to show genuine appreciation, and to be remembered.

* * *

By following these nine steps to manage discovery meetings, you'll be taking a systematic approach that gives you the best chance for positive results, including leaving with the vital information you need and a clear path forward to successfully close the deal.

9 Steps to Manage the Discovery Meeting

Step 1: Make introductions

Step 2: Build rapport

Step 3: Agree on the agenda

Step 4: Conduct a business-level conversation

Step 5: Listen actively

Step 6: Be strategic about the use of visuals

Step 7: Qualify the opportunity

Step 8: Confirm next steps

Step 9: Promptly take action

A checklist for adopting smart habits in your
discovery meetings is available in the Sales Essentials
Toolkit at the end of the book.

ESSENTIAL TAKEAWAYS

- Successful discovery meetings begin with introductions, rapport building, and an agenda.

- Conduct a business-level conversation by focusing on the prospect's goals, initiatives, and challenges.

- Listen carefully and pay attention to cues from nonverbal communications.

- Be strategic about the visuals you select to support your message.

- Objectively analyze whether this deal is a good fit for you and for the prospect so you can qualify in or qualify out.

- Save time to discuss next steps and collaborate with prospects to determine what those next steps are.

- Follow up promptly after the meeting and deliver on promises made.

CHAPTER

10

Communicate Your Solution Effectively

While initial discovery meetings are primarily focused on the potential buyer and emphasize our value proposition, subsequent appointments are opportunities to begin profiling our specific solutions to meet a prospect's needs. This chapter explores ways to communicate your solution so that it captures potential buyers' attention and meaningfully resonates with them.

THE BEST WAY TO TALK ABOUT YOUR SOLUTION

Before sharing some tips on what to say, it's important to reiterate what *not* to say. Don't lead your follow-up conversation by simply pitching your product. The discussion should be carefully molded to address the prospect's needs and challenges.

When it's time to start sharing your product knowledge, the following parameters will help optimize your conversations.

Customize Your Information

Align your solution to the potential buyer's needs and desired state, highlighting the benefits most important to the prospect. The secret is to arrange all the building blocks of your product knowledge to make the maximum impact with this particular prospect. That means starting the conversation with a recap of what the customer shared, confirming nothing has changed, and then using that information as an anchor to discuss your products as the optimal solution.

Use Language That Resonates with Your Buyers

Mold your conversations to fit your prospects by using words and phrases that appeal to their unique point of reference. Speak their language and be sensitive to their knowledge level—simplifying overly complex terms or including the technical details you sense they want.

Be Specific

Don't be the salesperson who throws out irritatingly vague statements like, "Our solution increases productivity and revenue!" Really? How can you prove that? How do you know that your solution was responsible for those improvements and not the other thousands of variables involved? If you're going to claim your product will solve the customers' problems, provide details to back up that claim.

Share Real-World Evidence of Success

You can tell potential buyers about your product features and benefits all day long, but it won't have the same impact as telling them how the solution worked for another customer with similar problems. Make it a priority to identify stories and facts from organizations facing the same challenges as your potential buyers. That kind of real-world credibility is priceless and memorable.

Research dating back to 1969 shows that telling stories rather than just stating facts or providing lists can dramatically increase information retention.[1] In that study, the average median recall of a memorized list was 13 percent, compared to 93 percent recall when the words were in story form.[2] Stark difference!

Other studies, including one conducted by Princeton University-based neuroscientist Uri Hasson, showed the brain of an individual listening to a real-life story synchronizes with the brain of the individual telling the story. In other words, they experience similar brain activity, which is known as neural coupling. The story establishes a mental bond between the speaker and listener as they form an authentic connection.[3]

Using stories is a great way to turn something abstract and complex into a relatable, tangible concept. If you can strategically weave these throughout your sales discussions, presentations, and demos, you'll paint a vivid picture of your products in action.

It sounds simple, but it really works. When the salespeople I train apply this concept, they're often amazed by the enhanced impact.

The bottom line? Providing evidence of your product's positive results in story form gives you a stronger edge.

Identify Realistic ROI for the Prospect

While storytelling is powerful, prospects still want to identify the quantitative impact your solutions could have for them. What's the potential ROI?

In discussions to pinpoint that, be clear about the variables and parameters involved, as well as the expectations (for you and the buyer) to achieve the desired outcomes. Measurable milestones and accountability should always be part of the conversation.

In addition, be careful about your language when projecting ROI. Rarely does one solution *cause* a change; it's more likely to be *correlated with* change. There are many other variables in the ecosystem that collectively contribute to an outcome, so overly ambitious claims reduce your credibility. Being too generic is also a problem.

On a related note, don't be afraid to course-correct prospects who inaccurately assume greater impact from your solution than is warranted. You'd be surprised how that honesty builds trust and shows buyers your true character. Those clarifications also help to prevent future problems. It's better to correct the misunderstanding now than to get a call from an angry customer in six months who says, "But I thought that was covered. . . ."

Here's my typical approach when course-correcting:

> I'd love to tell you the solution could do that but, to be honest, that's not something we can guarantee—and here's why. We can't control the external variables. No one can. However, I can share with you the benefits we've seen consistently with similar customers.

The main thing to remember? The ROI is useless if customers don't see value in reaching that point. Make sure you link it directly to the benefits they will experience.

Remember That Presentation Skills Matter

So far, this chapter has highlighted *what* to say when communicating your solution, but keep in mind that *how* you say it is equally important. We've all sat through school lectures that may have been filled with awe-inspiring information, but the delivery was . . . well, just dreadful. Boring. Monotone. Uninspired. The point is, if you're not excited about your solution, your prospect probably won't be either. Enthusiasm is contagious, so communicate with energy and confidence.

Recall from Chapter 8 the importance of making a positive first impression. All of those nonverbal communication components factor in when presenting your solution to the prospect. Your attitude, body language, facial expressions, and tone of voice are additional tools you can leverage to influence potential buyers and engage them in a compelling conversation.

If you're using any type of visuals to support your presentation, here are two recommendations. First, make sure the quality of your graphics is just as polished as your verbal presentation. You've probably invested quite a bit of time to get to this point, so don't let your credibility be undermined by a sloppy photocopy or poorly organized slides.

Second, don't overuse supporting visuals. Keep the emphasis on you. If the prospects are distracted by flipping through handouts or trying to decipher complicated charts, they aren't listening to you and making a connection with your message. Be choosy about what graphics you use and when to use them.

How to Optimize Your Sales Conversations

- Customize your information
- Use language that resonates with your buyers
- Be specific
- Share real-world evidence of success
- Identify realistic ROI for the prospect
- Remember that presentation skills matter

• • •

When you are strategic about communicating your solutions effectively to potential buyers—not only in what you say, but also how you say it—you elevate the quality of your presentations and increase your impact. That's always worth the extra effort.

ESSENTIAL TAKEAWAYS

- The quality of your communication in presenting your solutions to potential buyers will directly impact whether you close those deals.

- To be effective, customize your information and use language that resonates with your prospects.

- Be specific, share success stories, and identify a realistic ROI to give your message credibility.

- Make sure your presentation skills are top-notch and all supporting graphics elevate your message.

CHAPTER

11

Learn the Art of Collaborative Selling

When we're involved in complex deals, we're not the only ones who need to talk about our products and solutions in a compelling manner. The process of landing large, complex enterprise deals almost always involves a team of colleagues to help explain the solution and, perhaps, show the prospect the depth of support they can expect when working with us.

Sounds simple, but it's not easy to implement.

I admit I'm a bit of a control freak in my sales process. However, I quickly learned that I cannot, in fact, do everything myself. On the other hand, I'm simply not wired to let everything go and adopt a "whatever" attitude. Somewhere between micromanaging and "going with the flow," I found a sweet spot that allowed me to assemble a well-prepared, cohesive team for collaborative selling.

The benefits of using a team approach are pretty impressive. Research shows that deals involving multiple people throughout the sales cycle are 258 percent more likely to close than those with a single rep flying solo through the process.[1]

What's behind that? Having the right people engaged at the right time adds a level of credibility and allows each resource to demonstrate their domain expertise. Plus, it sends the message that the buyer will have broad-based support rather than just a lone-wolf salesperson. The impact of a group presentation also helps customers to more clearly visualize how your solution will help them drive their initiatives.

The key is being selective about the people you get involved.

Before I felt confident in my sales skills, I sometimes "unloaded the bus"—bringing my entire team into a meeting, including people who didn't need to be there. I wanted them by my side as an emotional security blanket, just in case! Not only did that strategy *not* add value, it made the poor prospects feel ambushed and intimidated. This technique did not work in my favor.

Now I follow these three guidelines for collaborative selling:

- Wait to get other colleagues involved until after the initial discovery meetings so you can determine which people will be most appropriate.

- Carefully choose the people on your team who can add value and help land the deal.

- Allow the prospect to see the rapport you've built with your team to demonstrate your success working in collaborative relationships.

THE ROLE OF A CONDUCTOR

When looking at the large enterprise deals I've won over the years, my role was less of a salesperson and more of a conductor—the one orchestrating the process. I wasn't playing every instrument, so to speak, but

I was making sure they were all integrated with precise timing to pave the way for a beautiful outcome. This is something that I also consistently see with top performers in my consulting practice.

I took the lead in building a relationship with the prospect and qualifying the deal. Based on the information gathered in discovery meetings, I determined which resources would add value and identified colleagues who complemented my strengths.

As team-selling conductor, I follow a number of standard procedures that I also train others on. These may be helpful in your collaborative selling efforts.

Fully Brief Your Team Members

Find a quick, efficient way to communicate the customer profile, industry, initiatives, and challenges. I populate a simple template that's easy to read and keeps me from leaving out any pertinent information. When appropriate, relevant research about the organization's competitors is included.

Share Your Knowledge

Provide your team with background information about the discovery meeting and any other calls that have taken place. What are the prospect's challenges? Is there a compelling event? What's the desired outcome? What things seemed to resonate? What roadblocks did you encounter?

Clearly Identify Roles

An important part of the conductor's job is to clarify the roles, responsibilities, and expectations for the people on the selling team. That coordination allows each key player to contribute in a way that complements other team members (rather than repeating or contradicting them). Creating that cohesive "package" requires strategic and tactical thinking, as well as sometimes navigating politics and bureaucracy. But your ability to assemble a well-coordinated team of resources will determine whether the prospect becomes a customer.

Demonstrating seamless teamwork can make a significant impact. In its 2022 State of the Connected Customer report, Salesforce found that 85 percent of customers expect to see coordination and consistent interactions among the departments in a vendor's company.[2] And a year earlier, a similar study found that, unfortunately, 54 percent report feeling like information is not sufficiently shared among marketing, sales, and customer service.[3]

Collaborate with Your Team

Take the time to strategize with team members about your approach and ask for their input. This collaborative thought process is critical in enterprise selling. Another study from Salesforce found that 60 percent of sales professionals believe their productivity increases by more than 25 percent when they engage in collaborative selling. If that's not enough incentive, 52 percent of those surveyed also report that making sales a team effort increased the leads in their pipeline.[4]

Communicate Openly and Effectively

As the sales process moves along, keep all team members in the loop—whether that includes information about key changes, emerging problems, big breakthroughs, or the ultimate win. Likewise, encourage every colleague to freely share information with you and the rest of the team.

Keep in mind that every person has a unique approach to communication. According to a 2018 report from the Intelligence Unit at the *Economist*, different communication styles are rated as one of the most frequent causes of communication breakdown within the workplace.[5] It's important as the conductor to recognize and accommodate these styles to achieve the best results.

For example, if you're trying to influence an internal stakeholder who tends to be data-driven, communicate using data, facts, and objective statements. Adapting your communication style to your audience increases the odds your message will be heard and accepted.

Once again, nonverbal communication also plays a big role. I always told my colleagues that I wanted their ideas and encouraged them to give me their honest opinions. Unfortunately, early in my career, my facial expressions and body language told another story when I heard them say, "Rana, I don't think this will work. Here's why. . . ."

My furrowed brows and crossed arms sent a message that didn't align with my cheery request for their input, unintentionally alienating quite a few people. Once I became aware of that disconnect, I worked hard to change it.

Provide Compassionate Feedback

The only way to achieve continuous improvement as a selling team is to be candid with your teammates and provide constructive feedback. If one of your resources is undermining your capacity for success (even inadvertently), you must speak up. But it's critical to address the issue with understanding and empathy.

It took me some time to capture the nuances on that. I always considered myself an empathetic person, but I might have been overestimating that trait. I was driven to close sales and expected everyone around me to match that same level of focus and commitment. I didn't always take their workloads and unique challenges into consideration.

In the context of collaborative selling, my enthusiasm to succeed became a little *intense*. Once when I needed to reach a colleague to get an answer for a prospect, I sent an email . . . then followed up with a text . . . then waited 30 minutes before I started calling.

My intentions were good, but the impact on my team was not. I had to step back and get some perspective. Prompt follow-up did not have to involve crisis-level chaos among my colleagues.

Just be clear about your objectives. If you've communicated effectively and empathetically with a colleague and still aren't getting cooperation, evaluate the cause and take action. You may need to find another resource. While that might be awkward, a weak link can put a deal at risk and increase the pressure for other team members to pick up the slack. Negotiate a personnel change in a professional manner that spares a relationship while spurring your potential to close the deal.

Show Appreciation

Landing a complex enterprise deal requires a team effort. If your colleagues knock it out of the park with a demonstration or presentation to your prospect, recognize their hard work and express appreciation. And if you win the account, include them in the celebration and make sure they know teamwork was the reason for the success.

There are plenty of ways to show gratitude for team members. A sincere "thank you" and a handshake are always welcome. But you could also reward their extra effort with a tangible item, such as a gift basket or certificate for dinner at their favorite restaurant. Those acknowledgments go a long way toward solidifying relationships with coworkers.

And here's more. Science shows that gratitude is associated with many benefits for both the recipient *and* the giver. These include physical and psychological boosts, as well as enhanced happiness and life satisfaction.[6]

The Role of Conductor

- Fully brief your team members
- Share your knowledge
- Clearly identify roles
- Collaborate with your team
- Communicate openly and effectively
- Provide compassionate feedback
- Show appreciation

USING DEMOS

Depending on the solutions in your portfolio, your sales process may include a product demonstration. If it does—and especially if that demo is complex—chances are that certain members of your internal team will be heavily involved in that. This is an opportunity for collaborative selling at its finest.

I will tell you from experience that demos can make or break you. Bad ones quickly put deals at risk. But engaging, compelling ones can excite prospects and allow them to really see the possibilities of embracing your solution.

Many of the same rules from your discovery meetings apply to the demo appointment: create a targeted agenda, use language that resonates with your prospect, avoid jargon, include attention-getting visuals, share customer success stories, prove the ROI, and simplify complex ideas.

Beyond that, following are some best practices to incorporate in your demos.

Make Sure Your Team Is Prepared

If someone on your team is delivering the demo, it's your job as the conductor to ensure they're prepared and on the same page. That involves customizing the information and keeping every point focused on the needs of the potential buyer.

You've probably already briefed your team members about the key players at the company. But before the demo is an excellent time to add your suggestions about the best way to approach them, what they want to hear, and what subjects to avoid. Those insights are critical.

I've listened to demos where the disconnects between the account executives and the sales engineers were obvious. It was apparent they didn't have a conversation before the demos, and the generic presentations were completely ineffective.

No matter who is presenting, start by developing a script customized to your audience. Some people may cringe at that thought, but let me explain. I'm not suggesting reading it word for word like a robot—absolutely not! Use it as a guideline until it becomes natural to deliver.

It all comes down to this: practice, practice, practice. And have a "Plan B" in case things don't work out as expected, especially with the potential for technology glitches in virtual meetings. You only get one shot at the demo; don't leave anything to chance.

Choose the Right Timing

Depending on the nature of your solution, you might find a demo is most appropriate in the second or third meeting. Occasionally it makes sense in the initial meeting if you've completed the proper discovery. The important thing? Understand the customer's world before you show them the cool features of your product.

Be Selective About What You Highlight

I've sat through hour-long sales demos that touted every single product feature and function without ever tying them back to the business outcomes. The prospect was overwhelmed and a bit bored. There were also times when sharing too much information created confusion. Be picky about what you want to discuss and highlight.

Think about turning the conversation from an inside perspective to an outside one. Instead of focusing on the products and features your company offers, present the demo in a strategic way that zeroes in on problem solving for the prospect. Be sure to mention the initiatives and challenges they shared with you in the discovery meeting.

Once again, storytelling can be a powerful addition to your demo. Be ready to share relevant stories in a conversational way. Here's an example:

One of the major challenges you shared with me is the impact of ongoing M&A over the years. You've been left with disparate systems that lack integration, making it hard to find that single source of truth. The ripple effect on decision-making and revenue streams has been difficult. And that's where I'll start the demo today. I want to show you how this challenge was handled by a comparable company—one that is similar in size, revenue, and number of acquisitions. We worked with them to address these problems and implemented a successful solution.

Now you've got their attention! The client knows you listened, understood their problem, and are about to show them a targeted response to solve it. That doesn't guarantee a sale, but it does give you an edge.

Include Data That Resonates with Buyers

Use the information gathered in your discovery discussions to calculate quantifiable outcomes. Be ready to present relevant data points that help the potential buyer calculate the risk and possible ROI. When you can combine this kind of data with your insights and some compelling stories, your presentation will be extremely impactful.

Create Opportunities for Engagement

Your demo shouldn't feel like a monologue or lecture. Keep it conversational and pause occasionally to let certain key points sink in. Prepare some targeted questions to ask prospects throughout the demo. That gets them actively involved in the discussion instead of passively receiving the information. The answers they provide can help you further customize your demos on the fly.

While it's helpful to have questions ready in advance, don't interrupt if your prospects have questions of their own. If they're engaged and interested, let their line of discussion take the lead.

Be Adaptable

Pay attention to prospects' body language and facial expressions during the demo to determine how it's going. If they look bored or confused, make changes in the moment that will get the demo back on track.

How do you know if it's not going well? If either you or the presenter is talking during most of the demo, that's a sure sign the prospect has zoned out. Quickly assess what might be causing that. Is the demo too generic? Is the presentation droning on too long?

Do what you need to do to reengage the audience. One indication that they are back on board is when they begin asking questions—a clear sign they're thinking through the solution and trying to figure out how it will work in their environment. When you successfully shift the emphasis of the demo to draw the audience back in, you'll be able to continue with a business-level conversation.

Address Any Concerns

In your quest to prompt dialogue during the demo, potential buyers may express some concerns. How your team handles those is very important.

Listen carefully and unpack the root causes of the concern. Hopefully your advance research has prepared you to handle the objections, but make sure you approach this as a discussion. Sometimes prospects just need to verbalize an issue as a way to discover it's not really a priority or it's not linked to driving their initiatives. If the concern is valid, be transparent about what you can and can't provide. Honesty and authenticity often outweigh the lack of a certain feature. Just keep business outcomes as the primary focus.

Avoid Bad-Mouthing the Competition

It's easy to let emotions take over when a prospect mentions your competition. "I can give you 10 reasons right now why our product leaves theirs in the dust!" But the reality is no one wants to work with somebody who bashes others.

Be sure you and your team members are committed to staying focused on your product, your differentiators, and your impact with your customers. Focus on showing value and refuse to mention any assumptions or unfounded allegations about your competitors. Take the high road and remain positive about what you have to offer.

A blank Collaborative Selling Summary is available in the Sales Essentials Toolkit at the end of the book.

• • •

The synergy of collaborative selling can be very powerful when you're trying to land deals that involve complex enterprise solutions. By mastering the art of leading cohesive and dynamic teams to support your sales efforts, you'll have an unbeatable advantage.

ESSENTIAL TAKEAWAYS

- Engage in collaborative selling that gets the right people involved at the right time.

- Position yourself as the conductor to coordinate the efforts of your sales team.

- Make sure your team members are well prepared to present demos that are succinct, customized, and focused on the prospect's needs.

- Work to keep the prospects engaged in demo conversations.

CHAPTER

Close the Sale

If preliminary meetings with the prospect have been successful, you've probably gone on to complete a thorough discovery process, shared insights, presented an overview of your offerings (perhaps a demo), and collaborated with the potential customer about how this solution could meet their needs. What's next? Closing the sale.

In this chapter, we'll look at five steps to take during the sale to help complete the transaction with a signed contract and a satisfied buyer.

STEP 1: PREPARE THE PROPOSAL

Developing a proposal demonstrates how well you listened to the prospect and how much you understand their business. Before getting started, though, make sure your opportunity is well qualified. Don't invest time on proposals, only to find out later the possibility of a deal is nonexistent. That can be painful.

When you're confident your account qualifies in, shift into innovative-thinking mode in your proposal development. Customization is, once again, critical for success, so let go of any notion that a standard, boilerplate proposal will work just fine. It won't!

So, how do you craft a specific solution that meets the prospect's needs but also sets you apart from competitors? That's the real challenge—and what will create real results.

Through the process of preparing the proposal, you may find yourself pushing the boundaries internally to meet the needs of your customers—in other words, coming up with creative ways to solve their problems. That can sometimes be met with pushback. "Sorry, as much as I'd love for us to win this deal, we just can't do what you're describing. We've never done it that way."

These situations are frustrating. You're trying to land a deal but are tied up in red tape and lack of flexibility. However, that doesn't mean you should shrug your shoulders and just give up.

As sellers, it's our responsibility to be advocates for potential customers. And sometimes that means being disruptors. If someone says your request isn't possible, try to unpack it and understand why. We owe it to our prospects to explore new options and fresh approaches, so don't be afraid to rock the boat internally as needed.

Of course, I'm not advocating being overly aggressive or rude. It's your responsibility to discover the rationale behind any restrictions. Are there legitimate reasons why the company can or cannot do certain things? Recognize when it's time to back off. But taking a positive, professional approach to pursue more innovative solutions within your company can deepen your relationship with your buyers and open the door for your company to gain additional opportunities.

Other ways to demonstrate your role as a customer advocate in the proposal development process include:

- Bundling a solution in a different way to help the potential client better serve their customers

- Streamlining reviews with the finance or legal departments to speed things up

- Making the delivery process more efficient to better meet the prospect's needs

While advocating for customers is key, it's equally important to be fair and realistic with team members. Collaborate with them and listen to their reasoning. Use the following guidelines to navigate those conversations:

- Talk to the right people internally.

- Don't just complain—come in with a proposed solution.

- Provide context by sharing relevant facts about the prospect and their needs.

- Explain the adverse effects of continuing with the status quo (for the prospect and for you, in terms of closing the deal).

- Find a win-win solution.

Once you've gotten internal agreement on a targeted and customized approach, prepare a proposal that is thorough, concise, straightforward, and benefits-driven. Most importantly, showcase your creativity in molding your standard solution to perfectly fit the prospect's needs.

STEP 2: PRESENT YOUR PROPOSAL

You've finalized your recommended solution and prepared a proposal. The next step is to share it with the prospect. Customers expect one, often saying, "Can you send me a proposal?"

Naturally we want to respond by saying, "Sure!" But here's my advice: *not so fast.*

How many proposals have you emailed that ended up with a no because they got lost in someone's inbox or were too complicated for potential buyers to wade through on their own? The risk is real! So what should you do? Throughout my career, I've learned it's always better to schedule a meeting (virtual or in-person) with prospects to personally share your proposals.

Those meetings allow you to explain your thought process, communicate stories, clarify pricing, justify the "why," and answer any questions. They also give you a chance to hear directly from your buyers and get their feedback. Use the input from those meetings to further modify written proposals so they better meet prospects' needs and overcome any objections.

Here are several ways to maximize the impact of your proposal presentation:

- **Create a setting where you have their full attention.** If you hand them printed copies of the proposal before you start speaking, they'll be reading ahead while you talk. Why kick off the meeting by giving them a huge distraction? At the beginning of the meeting, explain you'll be providing each participant with a detailed copy of the proposal at the end. In the meantime, keep their focus on you.

- **Don't start by unveiling your solution.** That might sound strange when the whole purpose of the gathering is to talk about what your company can offer. But if you do that, you've reverted to an inside-out view that leads with your product. Instead, recap the prospect's challenges and explain how those led you to design this offering. Connect their problems with your solution.

- **Weave in powerful proof points.** Reinforce the customer success stories and quantitative results you featured in your discovery meetings or demo. Remind them of the benefits that your solution can deliver and the problems it can solve.

- **Encourage open dialogue.** The more you engage prospects throughout the presentation, the more likely they are to be seriously considering your solution. When you review their challenges at the beginning, ask whether those still exist and inquire about the scope of the negative impact they are having. When discussing your product benefits, encourage them to ask questions or request clarifications.

    Those comments (or the lack of them) give you an excellent idea of how well the proposal is being received. If there are lots of questions and even some debate, you'll know the prospect is engaged!

While I strongly recommend scheduling a meeting to present a proposal before sending the document, there will be times when that isn't possible. The prospect might be too busy or facing a budget deadline. If that's the case, call and provide a synopsis of what to expect and schedule a follow-up call to get the prospect's reaction after receiving the proposal. A few hours after emailing the proposal, reach out through another communication method (e.g., text, call, etc.) to make sure the proposal was received and find out if the prospect has any questions. If you've already built trust with the prospect, taking a proactive approach like this will feel natural.

Occasionally prospects may refuse a meeting to review the proposal. In that case, take a step back and try to determine the motives behind that choice. Are they just using your proposal to check a box and show they looked at multiple vendors? Are they simply not interested? Or is there a chance the potential buyer didn't really qualify in? The answers to those questions will be extremely valuable in determining your next steps.

STEP 3: PROVIDE OPTIONS

Once you've shared your solution, give potential buyers some options. Research conducted several years ago by Tulane University professor Daniel Mochon showed something quite interesting. When consumers are presented with only one product option—even if they like that option—they are more reluctant to buy than when they are presented with multiple options. That's what Mochon called "single-option aversion."[1]

This concept applies to all types of sales transactions. Customers want to feel like they have choices. That gives them the control to select solutions that best align with their needs, budget, risk tolerance, and level of internal bureaucracy.

The advantage of choice does have its limits, though. If your prospect starts to feel overwhelmed by too many options, the conversation will likely fizzle into indecision or a no out of frustration. Research backs that up. Social psychologists Sheena Iyengar and Mark Lepper found that shoppers were 10 times more likely to make a purchase when choosing among 6 flavors of jam rather than 24 flavors.[2] Choice is good, but less is more.

Provide Prospects with 3 Options:

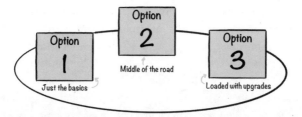

I recommend providing prospects with three options. Borrowing language from the automotive industry, offer them a no-frills subcompact, a classic midsize vehicle, and a luxury sedan loaded with all the upgrades. Explain how you landed on those three options and emphasize the value proposition for each one.

It's also important to be extremely clear on the differences among options to avoid any confusion. Clearly articulate the capabilities and the consequences of each choice.

With the options clarified and the value reinforced, introduce the pricing associated with your solutions. I feel compelled to add a comment here about presenting pricing information.

This part tends to make all of us in sales a little nervous. It's the moment when the prospect is either going to think, *Hmmmm, this could really work!* or *These people have lost their minds!* The difference in responses is definitely scary. And because of that, our previously flawless presentation skills can sometimes falter. Suddenly we're talking faster than normal just to get through this part. Our efforts to speak in the lower register of our voices and project confidence may fade, giving way to a higher pitch and a breathy sound that hints at the nerves seeping in.

Be aware of those tendencies, and work to combat them. If you've done a good job so far, feel confident about sharing the cost associated with solving their problems. Remain steady with your pace and pitch; don't let that throw you off. After presenting the pricing options, pause and give the prospect space to process the information. Don't be afraid of a little silence!

So, what happens if the prospect tosses a wrench in the conversation by talking about your prices being higher than competitors? Maintain your composure and remember it's likely not an apples-to-apples comparison. You wouldn't expect to pay the same amount for a Chevy and a Mercedes, right? The minute you start apologizing for the price, you become a commodity.

Reframe the conversation to focus on value and remind the potential buyer about the impact of the challenges they are facing. Describe your differentiators—including the customer experience you can deliver—and circle back to the problems you can enable them to solve, as well as the business outcomes you can help them achieve. Then ask if they have any questions.

In the vast majority of cases, prospects for complex, enterprise-level deals won't make a final decision on the spot. They'll likely have internal discussions and reviews at various levels. You might also have gotten feedback during the presentation that warrants an adjustment in your proposal. Get agreement on those changes and commit to sending those updates via email as quickly as possible.

Make sure you understand the prospect's internal decision-making process, and collaborate to set a deadline for a decision to be made. It's critical to establish a timeline for next steps to keep everyone on track. If you settle for an open-ended "I'll get back to you," the pressure is off and the risk of losing momentum is high.

In a famous article written for the *Economist*, British naval historian C. Northcote Parkinson advanced a theory now considered an important insight in the areas of public administration and management: "Work expands so as to fill the time available for its completion."[3] If you give me two weeks to finish a project, I'll take two weeks—even if I can actually finish it in six days.

Create some urgency around the decision. Schedule a follow-up meeting and send calendar invitations right away. That will cement the need for them to complete their internal process and be prepared—to give you an answer, come back with questions, or discuss alternatives.

STEP 4: NEGOTIATE EFFECTIVELY

By definition, negotiation skills are qualities that allow two or more sides to reach a compromise. Those skills involve planning, strategizing, communicating, and cooperating. How long does the negotiation process last? That depends on the complexity of the deal, the number of people involved, the industry, and whether an official Request for Proposal (RFP) is used.

While there are courses and books specifically on negotiations, here are a few guidelines that may be helpful.

Understand Your Potential Buyer's Process

Make sure you understand who is involved in the negotiation process. What are their roles and expectations? Don't be afraid to ask for clarification. Phrases like "Help me understand how this works on your end..." do that well. If multiple people will be participating, be sure each person has the complete background information and documentation.

Show Empathy

Always remember you're negotiating with human beings—people who have valid emotions, feelings, and motives. Sometimes that idea gets lost with all the contracts, legal language, and financing terms.

Stay focused on the potential buyers' perspectives and their concerns. How do they seem to feel about this opportunity? What are the implications for them, professionally or personally? Fight to find a win-win solution that will build trust and strengthen your partnership.

Recognize Options—Theirs and Yours

Remember, Your Prospects Have 3 Choices:

1. Choosing your solution ✓

2. Solving the problem a different way

3. Sticking with the status quo

As prospects are trying to decide whether to buy whatever you're selling, they are considering the alternatives and the consequences. Those alternatives include:

- Choosing your solution

- Solving the problem a different way (in-house or going with one of your competitors)

- Sticking with the status quo

That means having a solid understanding of the buyer's best alternative to a negotiated agreement (BATNA) as you embark on the negotiation process.

For example, if you're selling a training program, your potential buyer's BATNA may be using an internal enablement team to create and deliver the training. Tactfully asking some strategic questions could help you stay in the competition:

- "What type of resources do you have in-house to deliver this training?"

- "What's the skill level for the internal team in terms of developing content on this topic and delivering it?"

- "Is your internal team prepared to deliver the training within the allotted time frame, given their current workload?"

Understanding the prospect's BATNA will help you demonstrate why your proposal is a better alternative.

Equally important, knowing your BATNA gives you the wisdom to know how much you can give up during negotiations or when it's smarter to walk away. Nobody wants to negotiate from a position of desperation. If you simply can't help your prospect or if you determine that other deals in your sales pipeline would be a better use of your time right now, why keep fighting an uphill battle? Oddly enough, that knowledge gives you real negotiating power.

Demonstrate Your Commitment by Showing Flexibility

As customers, we've all been in situations where it seemed painfully obvious someone didn't want our business enough to help us get what we wanted. There's no flexibility and the person is not open to a discussion. Why partner with someone who won't at least try to meet you halfway?

If prospects make a special request, see if you can accommodate them. That might impact the price, but it could be worth it for them to get exactly what they want.

As you might expect, I still recommend searching for the proper balance between satisfying your customers and making a profitable deal for your company. Sometimes there's not an obvious answer, but clients appreciate the effort if you say: "Look, I'd love to work with you. And I want it to be a win-win for both of us. Let's brainstorm and figure out how we can make this happen!"

Here are a few tips for handling that type of collaboration:

- **Stay calm if your prospect brings up objections.** In fact, get used to it! If you end up landing the deal, you'll likely have a number of conversations throughout the partnership that involve differences of opinions. This is just another opportunity to show that you are willing to work together to find a solution.

- **Be sensitive to budget restrictions.** If the prospect's allocated funds aren't even large enough to accommodate your low-end proposal, how can you work with the budget they have? What can be trimmed? Or is it possible to implement the solution in phases, spreading the costs over a longer time frame that leverages multiple budget cycles?

- **Recognize when the best solution involves a compromise.** That may require you to sacrifice some things in the short term for long-term gains. Perhaps you approve the request to modify parts of the buyer's financing agreement and conditions in return for using their company as a marketing case study and reference.

- **Have patience with the process.** If your negotiation meeting involves a redlined contract, be transparent about the amount

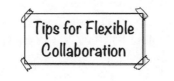

Tips for Flexible Collaboration

Stay calm if your prospect brings up objections

Be sensitive to budget restrictions

Have patience with the process

Recognize when the best solution involves a compromise

of time it will take for your legal department to review and return the documentation. Should an additional meeting be required to talk about the changes, schedule that as soon as possible.

The negotiation process may involve a series of twists and turns. But with patience flexibility, and empathy, you can skillfully collaborate to secure a contract.

STEP 5: MANAGE THE OUTCOME

At some point, the negotiations come to an end and the decision is announced. Hopefully, the answer is yes. But other times, great preparation aside, the answer is no. The prospect decides to go in a different direction.

The way we handle that outcome sends a loud message about our character and professionalism. The primary goal is to preserve the relationship—and the potential for sales success at another time.

Maybe the customer chooses one of your competitors but, six months later, realizes that was a mistake. Or perhaps your contact changes companies—or even industries. What if you land a new job?

By handling rejection with poise and demonstrating you still care about their success, you position yourself as the obvious choice to get the call the next time they are facing a challenge. Whether they bought from you before or not, the relationship you built may become the bridge to another deal in the future.

● ● ●

The next section of the book—After the Sale—provides many more details about how to handle the aftermath of the yes-or-no decision by the prospect. Chapter 13 includes strategies to set up new clients for success and turn them into loyal, long-term buyers. Chapter 14 takes a deeper dive on how to analyze your sales process after the fact to gain valuable feedback, whether you win or lose.

ESSENTIAL TAKEAWAYS

- Customize your proposal to meet the prospect's needs, and advocate for your potential buyer within your own organization.

- Present your proposal face-to-face (in person or via a video call), and lead with a summary of the prospect's challenges your solution addresses.

- Provide options in your proposal without overwhelming the prospect (three options is a good rule of thumb).

- Gather insights and feedback during the meeting to modify your proposal, and follow up by quickly sending any updates.

- Remain focused on the prospect's perspectives during negotiations, demonstrating flexibility, sensitivity, and a willingness to compromise when appropriate.

DURING THE SALE

Read the case study and use the information you learned in this section to answer the strategy questions that follow. (An Exercise Answer Key can be found at the end of the book.)

Jerry is a sales account executive with a company that provides cloud storage solutions for organizations in a variety of industries. After having back-to-back appointments all day, he saw it was about time for an initial discovery meeting with Lorenzo, an executive with a prominent healthcare firm in the midwestern United States.

Jerry hadn't had time to take a breath since he started his day, much less comb his hair. He grabbed a ball cap from the credenza and put it on his head. "This will have to do for today," he told himself.

He launched the Zoom meeting and was surprised to find Lorenzo and four others in the waiting room. He wasn't aware additional people from Lorenzo's company were joining the meeting, so he was caught off guard.

"Oh, wow. We've got the whole crew here," Jerry said. "I'm sorry for being late. It's been a wild day!" He sighed and continued, "I just can't seem to catch up. But thanks for joining me, and let's get started."

Lorenzo nodded.

At that point, Jerry jumped right in to ask Lorenzo a series of questions about his business. Lorenzo patiently provided answers, but as time passed and the questions continued, he took a deep breath and glanced at his watch.

"Jerry, with all due respect, the answers to all these questions can be found on the internet," Lorenzo said. "With a visit to our website or a quick Google search, you'd have access to everything you need. In fact, I just wrote a blog about the last topic you mentioned.

"So in the interest of time, let's skip ahead. Based on what I've told you, where do you see your company adding value for us? For instance, does your solution help us stay HIPAA compliant, given the most recent healthcare laws?"

A woman from Lorenzo's organization also chimed in, "Yeah, we need to know that. And have you worked with any customers of our size facing the same issues?"

Jerry had no clue who this person was or what role she played. He dodged that for the moment and answered them both: "Oh yes, I was just getting to that, but let me wrap up with one last question."

Lorenzo leaned back in his chair and crossed his arms. His brow was furrowed. He had no idea what they were trying to accomplish during the meeting, and he couldn't find an agenda to give him any hints. He answered Jerry's last question and hoped the upcoming value discussion would shed some light on the situation.

Unfortunately, Jerry launched right into a full-blown discussion of his products. He had spoken for several minutes about the amazing features and functions with great detail when Lorenzo interrupted him.

"But how does this apply to my business needs?"

Jerry almost seemed confused by the question. As he paused for a moment, he noticed one of the Zoom attendees had already logged off. He tried to stumble his way through an explanation that connected his products to their initiatives, but it was filled with inaccurate assumptions and vague statements.

Lorenzo cut in once again. "Jerry, it's the top of the hour. I need to switch to my next meeting. Thanks for your time."

Jerry quickly replied, "Sure! I'll send you a few white papers about our solution, and then we can coordinate next steps through email."

Lorenzo responded with a lukewarm, "Sounds good," and left the meeting.

STRATEGY QUESTIONS

1. What is Lorenzo's first impression of Jerry? *(timing, attire, attitude)*

2. What mistakes did Jerry make when starting the meeting?

3. What changes can Jerry make to improve the quality of the discovery conversation?

4. What should Jerry have noticed about Lorenzo's body language?

5. What would you have done differently to end the meeting?

CHAPTER

13

Set Up Accounts
for Success

I was in the Atlanta airport on my way home after a long week of traveling. Approaching the gate, I heard my phone ping. I had been waiting all day for news about a deal I'd pitched and felt a rush of hopeful anticipation. Sure enough, a quick glance at my phone confirmed it was an email from that prospect.

While other passengers were busily boarding the plane, I stopped right where I was—completely oblivious to everything around me. I anxiously scrolled through the email. Then I saw it. The approval. The contract. The crazy number of zeroes at the end of the purchase order (PO) amount.

Simultaneously stunned and thrilled, it took every bit of self-control I had not to scream at the top of my lungs and do an embarrassing "happy dance" in front of everyone at the gate. I needed to call my team and wanted to call my husband. But I just stood there, frozen—at least until I heard the woman on the intercom announce the final boarding call for the flight to Austin. I made my way to my seat, and I'm pretty sure I smiled the whole way home.

We've all experienced those unforgettable moments when we land a major deal. A proposal suddenly becomes a contract. A prospect becomes a customer. It's an amazing feeling—especially when we've invested a significant amount of time and assembled an incredible team to make it happen.

It's a great accomplishment, worthy of a celebration. And yet . . .

Our work is not done. The deal is only successful if we ensure that everything after the "big-win moment" goes according to plan. Let's look at the tasks required to set up your accounts for success after prospects say "yes."

FOLLOW THE BUYER'S PROTOCOL

You should already have a fairly good understanding of how the company's internal approval process works. But once that commitment actually comes through, ask the soon-to-be customer for detailed information to confirm your assumptions. Those questions might include:

- "What documents and paperwork would you like us to complete and submit right away?"

- "Do you require a Master Service Agreement (MSA)? And if so, who will be sending that over and when?"

- "With whom should we coordinate for any minor adjustments?"

- "Is there a preferred template for your Statement of Work (SOW)?"

- "Who will review the SOW and issue the PO?"

- "What's the typical timeline for that to happen?"

The answers to these questions help you align with your buyer's protocol and improve your forecast accuracy, as well as reduce the chances of any big surprises. As you wade through the paperwork process to get established in the buyer's internal system, there are several ways you can help keep things moving forward.

Support Your Sponsor

If your executive sponsors don't regularly onboard new vendors, be proactive about participating in the process. Share with them the typical next steps from your experience and describe what to expect. Most importantly, ask them to check with their internal resources to confirm or adjust your assumptions.

Get Legal Guidance

Your legal department will likely get involved if new customers require an MSA. Let your team members know the document(s) will be coming and provide a firm deadline for review. Once you get their changes back, don't be afraid to speak up if you disagree with some of their edits. It's your responsibility to make sure legal "fine print" doesn't paralyze the deal.

If you have substantial changes to propose after reviewing the paperwork, schedule a call that includes legal representation from your organization and the buyer's company. That allows for a group discussion as colleagues to iron out the details and avoid an endless, back-and-forth email chain. Sometimes small glitches can be resolved with a single phone call.

As the MSA is being finalized, develop the official SOW or contract. Your goal is to make the paperwork transition as easy as possible for buyers.

Manage the Glitches

Once the paperwork is completed and submitted, stay on top of the process. As the saying goes, "time kills all deals." Roadblocks inevitably crop up, so be proactive about managing and overcoming them.

Ask for confirmation of receipt after sending anything over to the customer. That might sound silly, but making assumptions can be a time-waster. I learned that the hard way as a rookie rep when my documents sat for a week unread in a spam folder. I've also waited patiently for a response, only to find out my customer was on vacation.

To keep things moving, have regular status updates with your contact and be prepared to route critical paperwork to other authorized signers as needed. When working on required documents, I usually ask several questions:

- "Will you be out of the office in the next few weeks? I'm happy to work around your schedule."

- "Do you use automated systems to route approvals, or is it all done manually through email?"

- "Are you heading into a busy time (end of quarter, end of fiscal year)? How might that impact the flow of paperwork and approvals?"

While on the subject of glitches, let's talk about a major one.

You're waiting for the SOW to be signed and the PO to be issued when your executive sponsor tells you she has accepted a new job with a different company. If you get the luxury of advance warning, that's proof you've developed trust and rapport with her. Ideally, she helps to complete the process before leaving or puts the pieces in place to make sure the deal doesn't fall apart.

The best insurance policy to prevent that loss is building relationships with additional stakeholders on the customer side. Commit to having regular contact with people beyond your executive sponsors and be sure to communicate the value of your solutions every chance you get. The day may come when you really need their support.

But what about the worst-case scenario? Your customer simply disappears—no response to emails or phone calls. You find out later he or she has left the company.

How should you handle that?

First, identify the person's replacement. Hopefully he or she has already been involved in the sales process along the way. If not, recognize you may need to step up and justify the proposed partnership . . . again.

I remember waiting on the PO for a strategic deal and finding out my executive sponsor had just gotten a new boss. Rightfully so, the new manager wanted to evaluate all the initiatives under way. I had worked hard to secure the deal, so this wrinkle made me nervous and, frankly, I was annoyed about the timing.

After processing my frustration, I scheduled a meeting with the manager. I started the discussion from the beginning, conducted a full discovery, aligned my solution with the company's priorities, and shared the solid business case. Thankfully, the deal went through, as planned.

That brings up an essential point. Relationships might be critical for closing deals, but things can also change quickly. On the upside, nothing makes a stronger case than selling value and objectively showing how your products can improve the company's business outcomes. Even if you're facing a personnel glitch, value can still save the day.

ORCHESTRATE A
SEAMLESS HANDOFF

Creating a positive customer experience is a task that starts before your initial discovery meeting and continues long after you've moved on to other deals. You, as the salesperson, play a pivotal role in that. If you create a seamless handoff to the implementation team and make sure they have everything they need to serve the customer, you'll pave the way for higher satisfaction, better retention, and potential opportunities for upselling and cross-selling.

So what does this process look like?

A seamless handoff to the implementation team paves the way for higher satisfaction, better retention, and potential opportunities for upselling and cross-selling.

Coordinate with Your Internal Team

First, inform all key stakeholders in your organization about the win and provide each with a packet of information to accelerate their learning curve about the new customer's business. Packets should include:

- Detailed scope of the project

- Goals, initiatives, and expectations of the buyer's organization

- Biographies of the key players for the customer, including personalities, communication styles, preferences, pet peeves, and quirks

- Expectations for internal team members

- Onboarding process outline (installations, training, development of support teams, time for additional discussions)

Schedule a meeting to review the handoff packet. Taking a hands-on approach to recap and educate team members about the customer and project details will help them build rapport more quickly and avoid any missteps that may put the account at risk. Be sure they understand exactly what has been discussed so far to ensure their language doesn't contradict any conversations you've already had with the new customer.

It's also critical to clarify the rules of engagement for servicing the account. Let team members know you trust them to do their jobs and won't get in the way. On the other hand, be transparent about your role moving forward and explain your intent to maintain ongoing contact with the buyers. The goal is not to secretly check up on them. You are simply staying connected to help deepen those professional relationships and, potentially, open the door for additional sales or referrals in the future.

Most importantly, let the implementation team know you are available to consult or answer questions any time. By creating a culture where the team knows they can come to you for clarification about a deal you sold, you'll be adding a layer of security to ensure your buyers are happy and getting exactly what you promised before they signed the contract. You'll also be setting up your team for success.

Facilitate Introductions for Your Buyers

Your new customers have been working with you extensively throughout the buying journey, and you've likely developed a sense of trust and rapport with them. They may have some underlying concerns about letting go and working with others in your organization. Assure them they're in good hands and take steps to help them develop solid relationships with new contacts at your company.

The best way to do that is to schedule a meeting to introduce your buyers to your implementation team. They may have already met some of your colleagues, but this is a great way to bring everyone together. It's also an opportunity to begin building a bridge toward the new phase in the relationship, while also discussing the all-important next steps in the onboarding process.

COMMUNICATE REGULARLY

Even though you've made the seamless handoff to your implementation team, communicating regularly with your customers is a smart investment of your time. Don't go dark on them! Following are some best practices to help you keep in touch with current buyers.

Strengthen Your Status as a Trusted Advisor

Check in with your customers regularly, including your contacts at multiple levels of the buyers' organizations (if appropriate). This is critical during the implementation phase. Naturally, you'll want to follow your company's engagement model, but it's also valuable to look at it from a personal perspective.

You've already developed a relationship with the buyers during the sales process, especially with complex deals that have long sales cycles. If things aren't going as well as they should during implementation, the buyers may feel more comfortable telling you about any problems. Staying connected with your customers gives you a chance to course-correct before frustration sets in.

In terms of ongoing contact, make those conversations more strategic by staying up to date with what's happening in their businesses and industries. Engaging in discussions on these topics helps reinforce that you are knowledgeable and attentive.

It's also essential to continue offering value. Research from global sales consultants at Challenger (formerly CEB) indicates about 53 percent of customer loyalty is driven by the sales experience. This includes insights, unique perspectives, and ongoing advice from sellers and related suppliers.[1]

Take the time to share the trends you are seeing and the implications of any changes you've detected on the horizon. Be responsive in answering questions they might have or addressing challenges that crop up. Ask them if there's anything else they need from you.

A final way to position yourself as a trusted advisor is to be the person who informs them about any pertinent changes within your organization. Whether that involves new products or a critical shift in senior leadership, hearing the news from you shows them you consider them a valued partner.

Maintain a Personal Connection

Business contracts aside, you have hopefully developed relationships with your buyers on a personal level. You've gotten to know something about their lives and career aspirations during your conversations. Use that knowledge! Continue investing in those relationships and express interest in what's going on with them.

This is another area where using platforms like LinkedIn can help you proactively identify any strategic changes happening with your buyers. Have they recently won an award or received a promotion? Along with more complex responsibilities and initiatives, a higher-level position usually comes with a bigger budget. Finding out about the new role can give you some clues about additional opportunities.

This also applies if your customer lands a new job at a different company. Being aware of the change lets you be proactive about extending your business relationship to the new organization.

Similarly, do you know what's happening with your customers from a personal standpoint? People love to be asked about things really important to them: their most recent vacation, their new baby, a new hobby they're enjoying, or an adult child who just got married.

I typically keep high-level personal notes about my customers under their contact names in the notes section of my iPhone. For instance, after having lunch with a prospect, I might jot down a few things I discovered during our time together: two kids, running the Boston Marathon, loves to cook. I then use those notes to refresh my memory before our next contact, which allows me to ask personalized questions: "How are the kids doing?" "Still training for the marathon?" If I know a buyer's birthday, I also add a reminder in my calendar so I can acknowledge the occasion.

When you take time to document these details and use them in your conversations, you'll reap the rewards. Your buyers will see that you care about them beyond the commissions they represent. You'll build stronger connections. And the discussions you subsequently have are more likely to include expansion opportunities.

Another important personal touch is thanking them for their business whenever possible. That helps make the connection feel like a relationship instead of a transaction.

Business professors and researchers Andy Fred Wali and Bright C. Opara conducted an interesting study about the impact of having a customer appreciation strategy.[2] They found that expressing gratitude to buyers directly influenced loyalty. As a seller, you should be part of the appreciation strategy.

Show your appreciation by simply thanking them in person or sending a thank you note. Sometimes the impact can be tangible. For example, a business owner once asked his reps to call their list of customers and just thank them sincerely for their business. No script. Just an authentic, warm thank you. A few weeks later, orders from those customers jumped by 10 percent.[3]

Expressing gratitude isn't just nice and polite; it's a great business strategy for a salesperson who wants to be seen as someone who can connect with others on a personal level. I follow that advice on a regular basis and encourage the people I train to do the same.

Reinforce Your Messages About Results

During the sales process, you and the customer identified and agreed on a tangible set of outcomes to be generated by your solution. Set up quarterly review meetings with your buyer and additional stakeholders to review the progress and results. Then use any data provided by the customer to update your success metrics and ROIs. As you refine those, make sure your executive sponsor has the latest information and can clearly articulate the positive impact of your solution for any high-level decision makers who might inquire.

In fact, I recommend creating a few slides your executive sponsors can use internally to continuously sell the value of your initiatives. Integrate quantitative and qualitative data, and use compelling visuals to tell the story. These can be powerful tools if your sponsors attend monthly leadership meetings and need to provide status updates.

Does this make a difference? Yes!

You might have sold the deal, but the competition for budget dollars continues. In addition to outside competitors, there will inevitably be people within the organization trying to poke holes in your solution with hopes of redirecting some of that funding for their own agendas.

If you want your program to remain in place, make sure your representatives on the buyers' side are always armed with information about tangible outcomes of your offering. That's particularly important for customers implementing your solution in a phased approach. Be deliberate about ensuring interim milestones are being reached so subsequent phases can proceed as planned.

Review these milestones with the customer and, if performance is falling short of the goals you originally set, work with them to evaluate whether modifications need to be made. If changes are required, collaborate to come up with a solution.

Sometimes the response may involve an adjustment in your offering. Other times, expectations may need to shift based on external factors beyond your control. Either way, be transparent about your analysis and keep the focus on generating the best possible results for the customer. This emphasis will demonstrate to the buyer that you are serious about producing business outcomes and meeting their expectations.

Maintain a Multichannel Presence

Your quarterly reviews and strategic conversations with customers are best received against a consistent backdrop of communications that give you an ongoing presence in their world.

That means continuing to show up in their newsfeeds on social media. Share pertinent articles with your insights, and comment on their posts whenever possible. You can also use email and phone calls to connect and reengage. As time permits, schedule in-person visits to further build the relationship and uncover additional opportunities.

When you participate in industry conferences or trade shows, see if your customers are attending. If not, extend an invitation! And make sure to schedule some one-on-one time with them during the event.

By getting creative and maintaining a presence, you use ongoing, multilayered communication designed to strengthen your business relationships.

PRIORITIZE RETENTION

While it might seem odd to start worrying about customer retention when you're still setting the buyer up for success, consider these statistics.

According to a study reported in the *Harvard Business Review*, more than 40 percent of B2B buyers second-guess their purchases after signing the contract.[4] Yep, buyer's remorse can creep in fast.

A report from Gallup paints another gloomy picture. This study found that 71 percent of customers surveyed are ready to abandon a current vendor at a moment's notice. If something better comes along, they may take it.[5]

There's a lesson in there you absolutely don't want to miss.

Even if the ink on the contract is still drying, retention needs to be a top priority for you and your team. Full stop. I understand that some companies have customer success managers and renewal teams that are integral in the post-sale adoption and retention strategy. But don't drop the ball on your end. Stay close to your team members and collaborate on strategies to ensure adoption and retention.

I've seen sales reps overlook this concept many times over the course of my career. They are preoccupied by celebrating the big win or get too comfortable with a large strategic account. They build alliances with a few key people who then leave the company or switch departments. These reps only reach out at renewal time, so the relationship starts to feel more transactional. They aren't paying close attention to competitive advances or innovative new offerings. Then, seemingly out of the blue, the account slips away. They feel blindsided.

That can be a painful and expensive oversight.

A *Harvard Business Review* study indicates it's 5 to 25 times more expensive to bring in a new customer than to keep an existing one.[6] And following the Pareto principle (also known as the 80–20 rule), we can assume 80 percent of your results are caused by 20 percent of your activities. Likewise, 80 percent of a company's profits typically come from just 20 percent of its existing customers. Losing a major client can be disastrous, for the salesperson *and* the organization.

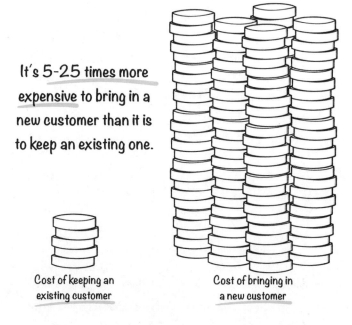

It's 5-25 times more expensive to bring in a new customer than it is to keep an existing one.

Cost of keeping an existing customer

Cost of bringing in a new customer

Source: Amy Gallo, "The Value of Keeping the Right Customers," *Harvard Business Review,* October 29, 2014, https://hbr.org/2014/10/the-value-of-keeping-the-right-customers.

The translation? Our current buyers are like gold mines we need to protect at all costs. Even if we're metaphorically handing them off to the implementation team, we need to prioritize retention and maintain our role in keeping the relationship alive over the long term.

Stay in touch, deliver on promises, and don't let buyers fade into the background.

ESSENTIAL TAKEAWAYS

- Confirm the internal approval process and timeline with your new customer.

- Inform all internal key players about the upcoming contract that requires their input and review.

- Be diligent about following up to make sure all paperwork is completed, the contract is signed, and the purchase order is issued.

- Orchestrate a seamless handoff by ensuring your team members have comprehensive information about the new customer and facilitating introductions to key players.

- Communicate regularly with your contacts using multiple channels to maintain your relationship as a trusted advisor, address any concerns, and uncover new opportunities.

- Arm your executive sponsors with data about results so they can sell the value of your solution internally.

- Collaborate with your implementation team to ensure adoption and retention.

CHAPTER
14

Analyze the Sales Process

Whether you land a deal or lose it, it's tempting to quickly move forward to onboard the account or pursue other opportunities.

But, I encourage you to hit pause and gather some specific feedback about the experience (positive or negative) that you can use to improve your future sales process. It takes effort to gather the right input, but it can help you grow as a salesperson. By identifying some critical issues to either intentionally repeat or avoid, you'll win more deals and stay ahead of the game. Knowledge is power!

Let's get the worst-case scenario out of the way first.

DEBRIEFING AFTER A LOST DEAL

We know we can't win 'em all. As sellers, the challenge for us is to stop thinking of these experiences as "losses" and, instead, classify them as opportunities to learn something valuable.

Get Input from Your Internal Team

I know what you're probably thinking: *Sounds like the perfect recipe for a gripe session.* Admittedly, emotions may run high in these meetings because of disappointment or frustration. Losing stinks! But it's your responsibility to keep things focused and make sure the conversations are productive.

Kick off the meeting by concentrating on what went well and would be worth replicating in the future. Those takeaways can be extremely helpful moving forward, and they set a productive tone for the rest of the discussion.

When it's time to sort out any mistakes or missteps, do your best to create an open forum for discussion about problems that need to be avoided with the next opportunity. Encourage people to share their thoughts and opinions. With that said, use your influence as the facilitator to curtail any passive-aggressive finger-pointing that might sabotage the positive atmosphere.

Remain solution-focused. Were there any red flags missed on qualifying the customer? Was this customer not the right fit? Did the solution not properly align with the buyer's needs? The key is to come away with a better "warning system" for future deals.

In some instances, you may have been so invested in a deal that you're feeling emotional about the loss. To get candid feedback regarding your role, consider enlisting the help of an objective facilitator during the debriefing session. That will enable you to gather the needed input without allowing your tone of voice to give away your opinions. The same thing also goes for your nonverbal communication. Your request for honest feedback may not be taken seriously if your body language is screaming, "We would have won the deal if you'd done your job!"

STEP BY STEP: HOW TO STRUCTURE
A DEBRIEFING SESSION

These guidelines will help you maximize your time and generate the best outcomes with internal debriefing sessions:

1. Schedule the meeting at a convenient time and invite key players.

2. Ask attendees in advance to write down their impressions of what went well and what did not to avoid groupthink in the meeting.

3. Consider each stage of the sales process, and encourage open discussion.

4. Make sure everyone present has a chance to participate.

5. Populate a template to summarize the areas of strengths and weaknesses as identified by the team (available in the Toolkit section).

6. Work collaboratively to correct processes and systems rather than blaming specific people or departments for any mistakes mentioned.

7. Develop a solid action plan that incorporates the findings from your discussion.

Even if you conduct world-class debriefing sessions, nothing will change without comprehensive follow-through. Without follow-through, the next time you plan a meeting, key players are likely to pass on attendance. They don't have time for all-talk-no-action meetings. Make sure the strategies discussed are thoroughly implemented, and communicate regularly with team members on progress updates.

Meet with the Prospect to Get Feedback

Some of the best lessons I've learned in my sales career came from hard conversations with prospects who told me no. Their candor—and my ability to accept constructive criticism graciously most of the time—allowed me to make targeted improvements and up my game. Those discussions not only helped me grow as a seller, but they showed the prospect something about me as a person. I was genuinely interested in helping them solve their problems, building a relationship with them, and honing my craft.

Even if I didn't win the business, the fact that I liked and respected them did not change.

Admittedly, talking about a loss isn't easy. I certainly didn't look forward to those humbling conversations but knew they were necessary. And if handled the right way, those learning experiences can produce benefits.

The most important thing about scheduling time to talk with prospects after lost deals is to make it clear you're not trying to change their minds. You just want them to be transparent and share their honest perceptions about the process—what went well and what you could have done differently. Let them know you respect their opinions and want candid feedback to aid in your own professional development.

Sometimes you'll uncover errors that you'll know not to make the next time. Don't get defensive. Just be grateful your prospects were willing to disclose that information. They're doing you a favor! Once you know the reason behind the loss, apply what you learned to the next deal. Be sure to also share any pertinent information with your internal team.

A piece of advice on this. If your prospect mentions mistakes made by specific departments or people in your organization, don't fire off harshly worded emails casting blame and copying three levels of managers. Remember there are always two sides to the story. Instead, use a calm and disciplined approach to discuss your findings. Share the facts provided by the prospect with your team, clarify what happened, ask for insights, and patiently discuss how to prevent those mistakes in the future.

You may discover the errors were due to faulty processes or systems rather than certain individuals. Maybe you'll identify an important skill gap that needs to be closed or an opportunity to clear up a frequent source of miscommunication. This is valuable information that might be lost if you allow your emotions to take over.

In other instances, you'll find out your inability to land the deal wasn't really about you at all. It just wasn't the right product, the right time, or the right price.

Regardless of what you discover in your debriefing session, keep the focus on the relationship you've developed with the prospect. It's not uncommon to win deals with someone who initially turned you down. Continue building trust and adding value. If another opportunity to pitch this person arises, you'll have the foundation of a great relationship.

DEBRIEFING AFTER A DEAL
YOU LANDED

The same philosophy about analyzing the sales process applies even if you walk away with a successful deal. Talk to your internal team members for their input, and then schedule time to talk with new buyers about their perspectives. Encourage candid feedback and express gratitude for their time and opinions.

Trust me, what you'll take away from those meetings will be just as valuable. I remember winning a large enterprise deal and thinking I didn't need any debriefing session. I must have done things correctly because I landed a new account, right? Well, not exactly.

Thanks to customer input, I recognized after the fact that my sales process wasn't as stellar as I originally thought.

I was working with the C-suite executives and assumed the executive vice president would be signing the SOW and PO. Since I failed to ask for specifics about their internal review process, I didn't realize the documents needed Board approval. That pushed the deal back until the next Board meeting. Which meant, despite my big victory, I had to adjust my forecasting at the last minute. Not a great way to end the quarter!

While I eventually landed the contract, the post-sale debriefing meeting still produced valuable feedback and pointed out areas for targeted improvement. Success should always be served with a healthy side of humility.

One of my favorite questions to ask during debriefing sessions with new customers is this: "Was there anything I (or my team) did that could have potentially put this deal at risk?" The answers you hear might include something like:

- "I felt overwhelmed by the amount of content you sent me."

- "I was getting contacted by a bunch of different people at your company, which made me question whether all of you were communicating properly."

- "There were times when it seemed like you were making the project more complex than it needed to be."

- "The demo could use some work. It was just too long and kind of boring."

If you see patterns or common themes emerging, use those findings to support your continuous improvement efforts.

It can be tempting to move on to other things after a win or loss. I've given in to that temptation a few times. But, *it's worth every minute invested to find out what went right and wrong during the sales process.* Don't let your busy schedule and looming deadlines prevent you from debriefing after every deal closed. Talk with your internal team. Talk with your prospect or buyer. The information you uncover may be the key to landing your next deal.

A blank Debriefing Session Guide is available in the Sales Essentials Toolkit at the end of the book.

ESSENTIAL TAKEAWAYS

- Meet with your internal team to debrief after deals (won or lost), creating an open forum for discussion about strengths to be replicated and errors to avoid in the future.

- Gain feedback from your prospects and share that information with your team.

- Ask new buyers if there was anything you did throughout the sales process that could have put the deal at risk.

- Use the information you gather to make improvements in processes and systems.

CHAPTER
15

Leverage the Account for Additional Opportunities

Imagine months have passed with your new customer. What's the possibility of increasing the size of that business long term? Much better than you might think.

What's driving that? After you've been working with them for some length of time, your current buyers know and trust you. You understand their challenges, initiatives, and processes. You're already in their accounting system with a PO on file. You've completed your onboarding, and you know how to navigate their organizations internally. If you have other products and services they need, buying from you is almost a no-brainer. You just have to ask.

Existing accounts are the ultimate low-hanging fruit in sales—ripe for the picking. But you'd be surprised how many opportunities we miss by not focusing on strategically growing these accounts. A study by Gartner found that "only 28% of sales leaders surveyed reported that account management channels regularly meet their cross-selling and account growth targets."[1]

So what can we do to leverage existing accounts and turn them into a lucrative source of additional opportunities?

CONTINUOUSLY ADD INSIGHTS AND VALUE

This one is simple, but it requires discipline to become a long-term task. Make sure you are regularly adding value for your buyers.

As mentioned before, customers want to work with reps who actively help them improve their businesses and achieve their objectives. A study by Gartner found the salespeople most likely to drive growth in their accounts are the ones who share insights and perspectives the customers may not have considered. These reps challenge their buyers with valid ideas and solutions and collaborate with them to execute strategies that move them closer to their vision.[2]

UPSELL AND CROSS-SELL

Account managers have a lot on their plates. It's easy to get sidetracked by a constant stream of tasks that need your immediate attention.[3] But if you don't make time to expand the business within your existing accounts, great opportunities may be slipping away.

As you continue to add value and insights for customers, be proactive about looking for options to upsell. Your relationships with your current buyers and proximity to their business operations combine to give you an exclusive view of what's happening on the inside.

It's still our job to be aware of what's happening in our customers' worlds. We need to use some of the same techniques we employed before our discovery meetings to stay on top of the news about their companies and industries. That includes setting up Google alerts, checking earnings call transcripts for public companies, and following major changes on LinkedIn. Those sources point to new opportunities that might otherwise be missed.

The goal of ongoing research is to identify any areas within the organization—even beyond the department that already engaged us—that might have potential for upselling and cross-selling.

Let's start with upselling.

Upselling

Perhaps your buyer signed up for a specific number of software licenses, and you've shown tangible outcomes that allowed the company to achieve an impressive ROI. In the meantime, the company announced an expansion into new markets with an aggressive hiring plan.

Based on their business needs and your results, you can schedule a meeting with your executive sponsor to propose upgrading their licensing agreement from premium to enterprise. That would allow them to roll out your solution to more users with the additional features they need. If you can highlight the benefits and show this move aligns with the company's strategic initiatives, your customer is likely to purchase more licenses.

The point there? It's much easier to add to a contract than to start from scratch.

Cross-Selling

Cross-selling is also an effective expansion strategy. This is where knowledge of your customers' organizations on a broader scale is quite valuable. If you've made the commitment to know what's going on in their worlds, you can uncover new opportunities just waiting to be tapped.

Suppose a customer recently acquired several organizations—a change that resulted in new challenges that can be addressed by a separate but complementary part of your solution portfolio. You can set up time with your customer to learn more about the updated priorities and discuss how you can provide value for people in different divisions of the company.

Strategic cross-selling further positions you as a strategic partner with your customers. It reinforces your willingness to collaborate and customize solutions designed to help them achieve their goals. And, perhaps best of all, it demonstrates your ability to be a full-service resource.

Strategies for Upselling and Cross-Selling

To make sure your upselling and cross-selling efforts remain top of mind, here are some strategies to employ.

Create Organization Charts with All the Key Players in a Buyer's Company

You can use specific online tools to create these charts or develop them on your own. Either way, this exercise can help you connect the dots and develop a strategy for growing the business within a particular company. For instance, you may have sold an enterprise-level solution to a general manager for one business unit within a global organization. Are other general managers facing similar challenges?

Develop Account Growth Plans

Bring together an internal team of resources to strategize ways to expand business with your current customers. What other products or solutions can you incorporate to better meet their needs?

You might even want to invite customers to join you in the planning process. If you've developed relationships with true partnership positioning, they will likely welcome the opportunity to collaborate with your team. Proactively working to identify areas of value can be extremely impactful.

Take a Systematic Approach to Building Accounts

Once you've developed a plan, use customer relationship management (CRM) platforms and other technology tools to make account growth as efficient as possible. These can provide data to help you make informed decisions and communicate effectively, as well as improve the overall customer experience.

Following this kind of systematic approach to expand accounts can give you an unbeatable edge. I remember being very excited when I landed a deal with a major company, even though the initial engagement was fairly small. Once I got my foot in the door, I made sure they were receiving the value they expected and then started looking for expansion opportunities. And why not? Doing business with me as an existing, approved vendor would make their lives easier.

I had already been onboarded, the paperwork was complete, and I understood the customer's internal system. Replicating my solution for other divisions was a simple way to expand the business and build it into a large account.

That strategy was very successful! I have used it on many occasions over the years with accounts that started small and transformed into huge enterprise deals. I've also seen it work with the top performers I've trained to use best practices in sales. In a nutshell, the growth strategy includes three components:

3 Strategies for Account Growth

1. Deliver on promises
2. Identify additional opportunities
3. Expand to other departments

1. Deliver on promises.

- Make sure your solution is performing to meet or exceed the outcomes originally specified.

- Schedule regular meetings to keep customers apprised of the project status.

- Give customers tools (visuals/slides) to update their leaders and teams about the progress and value of your solution.

2. **Identify additional opportunities.**

- Remain alert for compelling events and stay up to date on their businesses.

- Work to understand a customer's long-term vision and collaborate to create a compelling, efficient strategy to achieve it.

- Divide the strategy into phases and link those to a rollout of additional deliverables you can provide.

- Partner with buyers to sell the vision and your extended solutions to the appropriate internal stakeholders.

3. **Expand to other departments.**

- Look for opportunities to replicate your current solution with other departments or different geographic divisions with similar needs.

- Keep informed about any changes that impact your buyers' companies on a larger scale: expansions, acquisitions, new product launches, compliance adjustments, competitive moves, or legal complications.

- Extrapolate to determine how your solution portfolio could be the answer to any pain points they're experiencing.

- Work to expand your contacts within the company and try to gain influence with a broader base of stakeholders.

- Ask your executive sponsor or program manager to facilitate introductions to key players.

- Be deliberate about meeting with customers and new contacts face-to-face to build rapport on a deeper level.

- Make your primary customer contacts aware of conversations you are having with others throughout the organization to ensure transparency.

- Express appreciation and give credit to your original buyers for their support in helping to expand your business.

By following this proven approach for growing your accounts, you'll begin to see the bottom-line impact of your investment of time and effort.

ASK FOR REFERRALS

We talked about the power of referrals briefly in our discussion on prospecting, but this topic definitely deserves another mention. According to Nielsen's Global Trust in Advertising report, 92 percent of consumers surveyed report they trust their internal network for referrals.[4] But only 11 percent of reps actually ask for them![5] That disconnect is striking.

You've already done the hard part by asking for the business. If you've been diligent about keeping your customers happy and delivering on your promises, asking for a referral should be easy. Just make sure it's a standard part of your sales process. And when you do ask, you're tapping into the potential to gain additional business from inside or outside the buyer's company.

Internal Customer Resources

The obvious referrals to pursue involve other people within a customer's organization—someone from a different department or division or maybe another geographic location. Remember your sales journey to land the customer has given you an up-close view of their organization, their internal processes, and their goals. You have an enormous head start on your ability to serve others efficiently within the company. And if your contact recommends you to a colleague or coworker, you have instant credibility to begin the sales process.

One way to be proactive in this area is to create an internal referral network. This paves the way for additional introductions and makes it as easy as possible for people to help you connect with others in the company.

Last, pay close attention to the names of people mentioned by your buyers during your conversations. Find out more about them and, if it's appropriate, ask for introductions. That information will help you develop your organization charts and discuss growth strategies with your internal team. When the time is right, you'll have contact with other stakeholders who could become your next customers.

External Resources

Your request for referrals can also prompt your customers to provide names of people in other organizations. Perhaps they have contacts throughout the industry or beyond, many of which can be profitable. For example, your customers may be part of groups in which fellow members routinely ask around for recommendations on trusted vendors.

I've seen this happen on numerous occasions. If I've done my job to position myself as a strategic partner for my clients, somewhere down the road they pass my name along to someone with another company or a neighbor who works in a completely different industry. You never know how those connections will happen, but it's always a great idea to ask buyers to think of others who may need your solutions.

MONITOR RESULTS

The value of your existing buyers goes far beyond simple retention. If you've delivered results and developed trust as a partner, they can be catalysts to dramatically increase your sales. They are more likely to

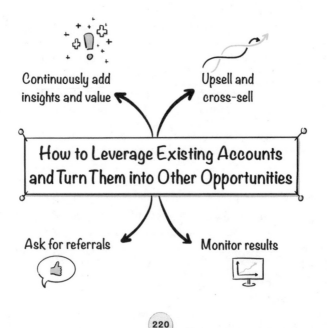

Continuously add insights and value

Upsell and cross-sell

How to Leverage Existing Accounts and Turn Them into Other Opportunities

Ask for referrals

Monitor results

send you additional business and feel more comfortable referring you to others. And if they leave for another organization, they may want to team up with you again. I've seen this play out many times.

The more you nurture existing accounts and work to strengthen relationships with key contacts, the more opportunities for new business you'll uncover. Never overlook the chance to expand sales with people who already trust you because that can increase your results exponentially.

* * *

As I wrap up this section, I can't help but reminisce about the friends I've made and the relationships I've developed by expanding deep into my accounts. Those connections mean more than just a sale or a commission check. I've created genuine partnerships with these people, and those friendships are priceless.

The personal and professional bonds I've made over the years have survived a wide range of life's highs and lows. Many of you who consider yourself "farmers" within accounts can probably relate to these experiences. I've celebrated with my customers after their promotions or congratulated them on their weddings or new babies. I've also been there during challenging times, in the midst of painful layoffs, bad quarters, divorces, or the internal politics of messy leadership transitions. The point is, I know them on a level that transcends our contractual agreement. That changes everything.

Professional partnerships that span good times and bad have the greatest potential to produce additional business. Working to stay connected with your buyers—as a vendor, colleague, and human—eventually pays off.

ESSENTIAL TAKEAWAYS

- Continuously add value and insights for your customers so they will welcome the idea of expanding your partnership.

- Identify opportunities for upselling and cross-selling within the organization, and develop a strategy to expand the account.

- Ask for referrals within the existing organization and beyond, requesting introductions when appropriate.

AFTER THE SALE

Read the case study and use the information you learned in this section to answer the strategy questions that follow. (An Exercise Answer Key can be found at the end of the book.)

Maria is a salesperson for a company that creates e-commerce platforms for retail chains. For nine months, she had been diligently trying to win the business of a trendy boutique with stores located throughout the southwest United States and a growing online presence building its customer base.

Her phone rang early one morning, and she was delighted to hear good news. On the line was Liam—her once prospect, now executive sponsor—confirming the decision to partner with Maria's company. She scheduled a meeting to talk about next steps before she started celebrating and high-fiving everyone in the office.

Maria knew Liam had been in his role for less than a year and didn't have much experience with onboarding new vendors. She was a little concerned about getting all the paperwork processed and making sure no one dropped the ball on the customer side. She also realized several members of her internal team were about to leave town for the holidays, and she wondered how that might impact the process of onboarding the account.

STRATEGY QUESTIONS

1. How should Maria structure the meeting with Liam to help avoid any hitches with the onboarding process?

2. What best practices should Maria follow in handing off the new account to her internal team?

3. How can Maria deepen and nurture the account relationship over time?

PART III

BEYOND THE ESSENTIALS

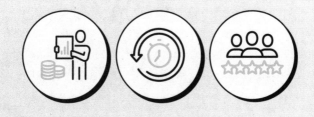

CHAPTER

16

Dealing with Rejection

Now that you've analyzed the sales process from beginning to end, you have the knowledge and context to move beyond the essentials. In this part of the book, you'll explore the psychological and emotional impact of having a career in sales. Most importantly, you'll gain some strategies to help you manage those factors for greater success.

It's an unfortunate fact. If we're in sales, we're going to experience rejection. Many times. We can't win a new account if we don't take the risk of pitching it—which comes with the potential for losing. It's part of the job!

Of course, that doesn't make it any easier when people hang up on us during a cold call, yell at us for interrupting their day, or tell us we lost a huge deal after working on it for months. The truth is, rejection stinks.

THE PSYCHOLOGICAL IMPACT

What makes it so awful? It has to do with our brains. For example, rejections that entail uncertainty about the future (such as potentially not meeting quota because of losing a large forecasted deal) can cause sales reps to experience anxiety and lower self-esteem. Plus, losses perceived to be unfair trigger anger.[1]

But the psychological impact of hearing no actually goes deeper than that. *It hurts.*

A study from UCLA's Dr. Naomi Eisenberger showed that the brain processes rejection along the same neurological pathways as when we have a physical injury.[2] If you hear colleagues talking about the pain of losing a sale, they actually mean it.

So, what can you do instead of wallowing in rejection? I have a few ideas.

COPING MECHANISMS FOR REJECTION

As someone who has faced plenty of rejection over the years (and observed others getting rejected), I fully understand the psychological ups and downs that come with a career in sales. With my experience, I've accumulated a list of strategies that help cope with the pain of hearing no. I am not a licensed therapist. If the pain of rejection overwhelms you, seek out the support of a qualified professional.

Here are six ways to help mitigate the psychological impact of rejection in sales.

Adjust Your Expectations

As mentioned before, the potential for a win is always paired with the potential for a loss. There are no guarantees.

Acknowledge that rejection is inevitable. You win some, you lose some. By adjusting your expectations to accept some percentage of losses, you put rejection into context. It's not a sign of failure and defeat. It's just a normal setback on the way to your next win.

Identify the Reason for the Loss

This coping mechanism requires an emphasis on the self-awareness discussed earlier. We have to move beyond the pain, frustration, and anger of rejection to analyze the situation calmly and logically. What went wrong?

Debriefing sessions can help you find the likely culprit or give you the satisfaction of knowing the loss was due to unrelated factors. Knowing puts you in control.

Don't Take It Personally

Easier said than done, I know. But here's one way to look at it. The reality is, sometimes our solution just wasn't right. The timing was off. The price point was out of reach. Or internal politics on the prospect's side presented a hurdle we couldn't possibly jump over.

Unless we acted like total jerks during the sales process, the rejection simply wasn't about us. Accept it and let it go.

An excellent perspective on this comes from Brenda Hudson, senior vice president of commercial sales, sales enablement, and learning and development at Insight Enterprises, Inc. "Especially with acquiring new customers, you're going to get lots of nos before you get a yes," Hudson explained. "Our best sellers look at no as feedback. Some take it as a challenge! Don't view rejections as a personal thing. Stay politely persistent and keep going. Don't let a no shut you down!"[3]

Stay Focused on the Long-Term Relationship

This technique has helped me overcome some of the biggest losses in my sales career. Just because a prospect says no today doesn't necessarily mean no forever. Things change. Budgets fluctuate. Competitors may fail to deliver on their promises.

If we've made a good impression on prospects and consistently added value—even after losing the deal—the door is never completely closed. Maintain those relationships and stay in touch.

Concentrate on the Next Deal

I've always believed there's a trade-off to everything we do. So, despite the pain of rejection, sometimes losing a deal can be a blessing in disguise because it frees us up to focus on landing another account.

If you've been diligently prospecting, you should have a healthy pipeline of leads that can now get your full attention. Make sure you have other options waiting.

Adopt a Positive Mindset

It's perfectly normal to feel down, frustrated, or upset when a deal we've worked hard to win is lost. But those feelings become detrimental if we allow ourselves to dwell on them for a long time. My approach is to feel the sadness and frustration for 24 hours—and then move on.

Give yourself some limited space to accept the loss, but then turn the page. This means eliminating any negative self-talk that tends to perpetuate the pain. I know I've been guilty of that in the past: *I feel like the biggest idiot. I've worked so hard, and I have nothing to show for it!* or *I can't do this anymore. I'm done!*

While adopting a positive mindset requires some mental discipline, it's possible to achieve. And, better yet, we can benefit by looking at our sales losses as opportunities for growth. What changes or improvements could we make to land the next account? What areas of strength could we lean into? Take what you learn and use it to win the next deal. A positive mindset can change everything.

Rejection Coping Mechanisms

Adjust your expectations

Identify the reason for the loss   Don't take it personally

Stay focused on the long-term
relationship

Concentrate on the next deal   Adopt a positive mindset

• • •

There's no way around it—if you're in sales, you're going to experience rejection. How you handle it will determine whether it tears you down or fuels even greater success in the future.

ESSENTIAL TAKEAWAYS

- Rejection is an inevitable part of sales.
- The brain processes rejection along the same neurological pathways as when we have a physical injury, so it does actually hurt.
- Coping mechanisms for rejection in sales include adjusting your expectations, identifying the reason for the loss, not taking it personally, staying focused on long-term relationships, concentrating on the next deal, and adopting a positive attitude.

CHAPTER

17

Protecting Your Mental Health

I'll be first in line to talk passionately about the many benefits of a career in sales. It's thrilling and profitable and exactly what those of us who thrive on a competitive challenge need in our lives. As I've mentioned before, I can't imagine doing anything else. And the excitement of teaching other reps how to sell effectively has been a major highlight in my professional life.

But I would be remiss if I didn't take an opportunity to talk about another angle of this career choice—something that goes beyond just facing rejection as discussed in the last chapter. By its very nature, a career in selling can have an impact on the broad spectrum of our mental health.

MY STORY

From personal experience, I know how the constant push to perform can take a toll. When I started my sales career, I was one of the first people in the office every morning and one of the last to leave. I worked nights and weekends, even on vacations.

I should probably point out that the only person who expected me to put in so many hours was . . . me. I placed enormous pressure on myself—lots of it. Working hard was ingrained in my DNA. My tireless work ethic came from watching my parents hustle to survive and being an immigrant chasing the American dream. I was simply wired to keep going and going and going and going . . . until I couldn't.

A freak accident that shattered my right foot stopped me in my tracks, literally and figuratively. I went from full speed to zero in an instant, and the contrast shocked me to my core.

I couldn't walk. I couldn't drive. The pain was excruciating. And the road to recovery involved surgery and hours of physical therapy. For the first time in my life, I was forced to pause, unpack, and reflect. That imposed time away made me look deep into myself and realize the pace I had established for my career was unhealthy and, even worse, unsustainable.

I'm not discounting the importance of hard work. I still wake up every morning with that burning drive to go after my dreams full force. But the accident did teach me something that changed the way I look at life.

I can't be the best possible version of myself as a seller and someone who trains other salespeople if I don't pay attention to my mental, emotional, and physical health. They are all connected. If I neglect one part of the equation, I can't reach my full potential in the others. Talk about an epiphany!

As a fellow sales professional, that's the piece of advice I hope you'll take away from this. It transcends the scope of winning deals. No matter how hard you work, commit to taking care of yourself on multiple levels—including your mental health. You'll discover that directly translates into being a better sales rep, a better employee, a better colleague, a better partner, a better parent, and a better friend. When it's all said and done, that's what really counts.

With that in mind, let's take a closer look at the impact of sales-related stress, the research on this topic, and solutions to prioritize your mental health.

THE IMPACT

Making a living in sales comes with some built-in pressure. Despite our success, we frequently experience:

- The anxiety of ever-increasing expectations to perform

- The fear of getting fired if we don't meet our quotas

- The disappointment of getting ghosted by prospects

- The erosion of confidence that comes with losing an account

- The aggravation of dealing with internal bureaucracies and disparate systems

- The stress of constant multitasking to keep customers happy

- The exhaustion of burnout due to the daily grind

Any way you look at it, there's an emotional price to be paid for working in sales. That's why I'm often surprised that the issue of mental health isn't widely and openly discussed with people who sell for a living. It is a real problem with serious impact in our industry.

I often wonder if it might get overlooked because salespeople generally appear to be confident, upbeat, and motivated professionals who can handle almost anything—like superheroes without capes. That's precisely why I believe the mental health of salespeople is a topic that needs and deserves a full discussion.

THE RESEARCH

Scientific studies clearly indicate that mental health is a significant concern for people in sales. In 2022, UNCrushed, Sales Health Alliance, and The Harris Consulting Group surveyed sales professionals and found that 63 percent reported struggles with their mental health.[1] The study also showed a strong correlation between mental health and sales performance: a decline in one caused a decline in the other.[2]

The research also uncovered an unfortunate domino effect in the industry. Top sales performers burn out. They leave. The remaining salespeople try to pick up the slack on the way to their own burnout. And the cost of hiring and rehiring keeps going up. In fact, a survey done in late 2019 by UNCrushed Inc. (a platform for mental health awareness) found that 67 percent of sales reps agreed or strongly agreed that "they are close to currently experiencing burnout."[3] I would venture to guess that number is even higher since the pandemic.

THE SOLUTIONS

Knowing that our jobs could possibly put our mental health at risk, what can we do to help protect our well-being? We need to make our health a priority.

Admittedly, I struggle with this. Early on, the concept of taking time out to care for myself didn't really fit into my constant-productivity mindset. But between my accident and plenty of experience, I discovered the direct connection: Without good health, my hustle suffers. I get it now, but I'm still a work in progress!

The ideas that follow can be implemented to help you maintain a positive, healthy outlook as you navigate the exciting world of sales. Once again, I offer these suggestions based on my experiences. But if you need more personalized support, I recommend reaching out to a mental health specialist.

Check Your Environment

When things get hectic, it's easy to keep putting one foot in front of the other and doing what we always do. Change is difficult, and the fear of the unknown can paralyze us. But stop long enough to look around and determine whether your environment could be endangering your mental health. Do you constantly feel stressed? Are the goals and expectations unreasonable? Does the workplace seem toxic? If you don't feel valued, respected, and appreciated at work, it might be time to consider a change.

Before accepting another sales position that could have the same problems (or worse), do your due diligence.

Think about the ideal work culture that allows you to thrive and perform at the highest level. Engage in self-awareness exercises to determine what environment fits you the best. Then search for an organization that aligns with your style and that structure. Review career sites like Glassdoor and Indeed to look for patterns in comments about the company culture in general and the sales culture more specifically. What pros and cons are people repeatedly mentioning?

During an interview, ask about the company's resources for onboarding and sales enablement. Do they provide the tools and training you need to be successful in selling their solutions? What support will they offer to help you ramp up and meet your targets? Be proactive about exploring this area.

Should you progress to additional interviews, do some research on your potential manager. Use sites such as LinkedIn to learn more about this person's leadership style and personality. You might even reach out to any shared connections for additional background information. It's a way to help you decide whether that possible working relationship would be a positive one.

Know Your Triggers

Be honest with yourself. Not meeting quota causes stress for all of us. But what other parts of your job tend to kick your anxiety into high gear? Here are some of the most common ones for salespeople:

- Being rejected

- Being micromanaged

- Not having enough downtime

- Not getting time or direction from an overly busy boss

- Fighting through internal politics and bureaucracies

- Wrangling dissatisfied customers

- Buckling under the pressure of an increased quota

If you're fully aware of these triggers and how they make you feel, you may be better prepared to manage them and minimize their negative impact.

Be Proactive About Counteracting Stress

We've established sales can be tough on our mental and physical health. Those triggers are out there! To survive long term in this profession, we need to get ahead of the game and be proactive about how we live our lives to help us withstand the negative impact.

- **Find time to eat healthy and get enough sleep.** I debated whether to include this reminder because it's such overused advice. But the reality is, many of us tend to gloss over these commonsense basics. We're on the road, attending conferences, working the trade show floor, or juggling back-to-back meetings. Food deliveries and late-night snacking can easily become the rule instead of the exception. Those choices can quickly undermine our ability to handle stress.

  From experience, I know the impact insufficient sleep can have on my performance and health. I remember being extremely sleep-deprived when I was writing my dissertation. Without even thinking about it, I touched the hot oven rack with my bare hands. The weirdest part of it? It took my exhausted brain several seconds to even recognize what was happening. We simply can't function well if our bodies aren't getting the rest and fuel they need.

- **Exercise regularly—or just move more.** With the rise of virtual selling, we can sometimes spend an entire day at our desks making calls. That lack of movement is harmful for our physical and mental health.

  To ramp up and build momentum, start by committing to 30 minutes of physical exercise daily. Mark that time on your calendar and consider it the most important meeting of your day—even if your schedule is packed and big projects are due. Exercise gives you the strength and stamina needed to be successful.

Practice gratitude. While that might sound like a cliché, there's a lot of wisdom and science behind it. Approaching the world with an attitude of gratefulness measurably improves our own mental health.

Be intentional about reflecting on the good things in your life—personal and professional. Look at what you have, what you've accomplished, and what is important to you. List those things on paper or say them out loud. Most importantly, actively appreciate them. I know from experience that the power of gratitude can make a huge impact on our mindset.

Have a positive support system. Surround yourself with people who regularly encourage you and provide honest feedback in a way that lifts you up, not drags you down. If you're around people at work who are notorious for infusing toxic negativity, recognize the impact that has on the way you sell and consider your options.

Celebrate all wins—big and small. It can take months to land a new account. But do you celebrate the smaller milestones along the journey? Taking a moment to recognize those interim achievements can give you a nice boost. Maybe you finally scheduled a meeting with an elusive prospect. Or you got an existing customer on the phone and generated real interest in a new product offering.

The job might not be done, but you've taken important steps in the right direction. Recognize that—it's good for your mental health.

- **Find something you enjoy doing outside of work.** Perhaps you enjoy golfing, painting, running, reading, volunteering in your community, or the guilty pleasure of watching a reality TV series. Whatever it is, find time to mentally "check out" and temporarily put your sales-related tasks aside. You'll feel happier—and the diversion is likely to make you more focused and creative when you return to your office.

Ways to Counteract Stress

Find time to eat healthy & get enough sleep

Exercise regularly— or just move more

Practice gratitude

Have a positive support system

Celebrate all wins— big and small

Find something you enjoy doing outside of work

• • •

Every career choice has its pros and cons, but I believe that working in sales has many more advantages than drawbacks. If you are proactive about protecting your mental and physical health, you can take control of your day-to-day experience, your income, and your future. I may be biased, but I believe that no other job gives you that professional power quite like the field of sales.

ESSENTIAL TAKEAWAYS

- The mental health of salespeople is a topic that deserves to be discussed and addressed.

- A career in sales may offer excitement and a competitive challenge, but it also involves emotions that may take a toll on mental health: anxiety, fear, disappointment, frustration, exhaustion, and stress.

- Salespeople can protect their well-being by making health a priority, being aware of their environment, knowing their triggers, and being proactive about counteracting stress.

- People who successfully manage stress in their lives get plenty of rest, eat a healthy diet, exercise regularly, practice gratitude, have a positive support system, celebrate big and small wins, and find something they enjoy doing outside of work.

18

Embracing Your Career in Sales

You've done it! You have now looked at sales from start to finish, walking step-by-step through the entire process—from doing research, prospecting, and preparing for discovery meetings to effectively using demos, closing deals, and leveraging accounts to uncover additional opportunities.

Although you explored each segment of sales in depth, remember there's a single thread that ties it all together. It's the importance of building high-trust relationships. In sales, that's *critical*.

I'm not talking about fluffy, emotional connections here. I'm referring to relationships that form through a salesperson's grit and hard work before, during, and after the sale. By consistently adding value and sharing insights. By being brave enough to challenge the customer's thinking. And by delivering on promises, even when things don't go as expected.

That combination of actions develops the bonds of trust and elevates a vendor relationship into a genuine partnership.

Remember, *people buy from people*. The high-trust relationships you work to develop with prospects will singularly define your success as a salesperson. I can't emphasize that enough. It's a cornerstone concept of my sales enablement programs.

People Buy from People

If you consistently build rapport, prove you have the customers' best interests at heart, and handle both wins and losses with equal amounts of grace and professionalism, you *will* become a world-class salesperson. That doesn't mean you'll land every deal. (You won't.) But it will change the course of your career long term and dramatically increase your overall win rate.

You now have the tools to make that happen—to close more deals *and* crush your quota! And if you apply the strategies and best practices you've learned here, you'll earn the type of reputation as a salesperson that will set you apart in extraordinary ways.

Thank you for investing the time to read this book and allowing me to share my expertise and experiences with you. I know your time is valuable, and I hope the information offered helps you achieve your objectives. Also, remember to check out the Sales Essentials Toolkit that follows for additional resources to support your journey as a sales professional.

Wishing you the greatest success as you work every deal, strengthen every relationship, and transform every customer into a loyal partner. Go get 'em!

—Rana

Sales
Essentials Toolkit

To help maximize the knowledge you gained from this book, I've provided some resources that support your growth as a salesperson. The components in this section include:

- Preparing for Discovery Meetings Checklist

- Managing a Positive First Impression Checklist

- Adopting Smart Habits for Discovery Meetings Checklist

- Following Best Practices in Sales Checklist

- Discovery Meeting Organizer

- Collaborative Selling Summary

- Debriefing Session Guide

- Sales Methodologies to Know

PREPARING FOR DISCOVERY MEETINGS CHECKLIST

Use this checklist to ensure you are fully prepared for productive discovery meetings with your prospects. Any questions marked no become your action items prior to the appointment.

	Yes	No
Optimizing Your LinkedIn Profile for Social Selling		
Have you updated your LinkedIn profile picture within the past year?		
Have you updated your profile headline to attract attention from your buyer persona?		
Have you updated your profile summary (the *About* section) to make it relevant to your buyer persona?		
Have you updated your roles and responsibilities (the *Experience* section), taking an outside-in perspective to resonate with your prospects?		
Have you included recommendations from your existing customers?		
Identifying Clear Objectives		
Have you identified the objectives of the discovery meeting in advance?		
Did you send the agenda to the prospect before the meeting?		
Did the prospect agree with the agenda?		

	Yes	No
Doing the Research		
Did you conduct a quick Google search on the company?		
Did you check the organization's latest earnings call transcript (if it's a public company)?		
Did you conduct a quick Google search on the prospect and any other stakeholders who will be attending the meeting?		
Did you review the LinkedIn profiles of the prospect and the other stakeholders?		
Did you check to see if you have any shared connections with the people attending the meeting?		
Did you search for any shared experiences or interests that might aid in building rapport?		
Did you identify relevant information you can use to build credibility and uncover opportunities during the meeting?		
Did you identify any potential pain points your solution can help to relieve?		
Did you identify the prospect's potential initiatives your solution can help drive?		
Did you develop a few relevant and targeted questions to ask during the discovery meeting?		

	Yes	No
Did you identify potential customer stories that may resonate with your prospect?		
Did you identify any insights or data your prospect may find of value?		
Confirming the Appointment		
Did you send a reminder/confirmation email to the prospect 24 hours before the meeting?		

MANAGING A POSITIVE FIRST IMPRESSION CHECKLIST

Answer these questions based on your *most recent sales meeting*. Any lines with responses marked no can be considered action items to help improve the first impressions you make in the future.

	Yes	No
Timing		
Did you arrive early to the meeting?		
Did you test your technology upon arrival to ensure it would work?		
Attire		
Did you dress appropriately for the audience, environment, expectations, and meeting objectives?		
Starting Point		
Did you start the meeting with introductions?		
Did you begin building rapport up front?		
Did you share the agenda with the prospect in advance?		
Voice		
Did you project confidence in your voice?		
Did you balance/adjust your pitch and inflection to suit the situation?		

	Yes	No
Did you follow the prospect's pace and volume as a guideline for your own speech?		
Facial Expressions		
Did you make natural, culturally appropriate eye contact with the prospect during the meeting?		
Were your facial expressions aligned with your words?		
Body Language		
Did you lean in slightly to shake hands?		
Did you stand up tall during the introductions and the presentation?		
Did you have good posture without looking stiff?		
Did you have an open stance with relaxed arms?		
Did you use natural hand gestures to support your own words?		
Did you nod gently as the prospect spoke?		
Attitude		
Did you smile appropriately throughout the meeting?		
Did you project positive energy?		

	Yes	No
Virtual Office		
Did you turn on your webcam to create a face-to-face interaction?		
Was your webcam set up just above eye level?		
Did you have some form of lighting in front of you?		
Did you use a simple background and remove clutter?		
Did you use a headset to maximize your ability to hear the prospect during the meeting?		

ADOPTING SMART HABITS FOR DISCOVERY MEETINGS CHECKLIST

Use this checklist to remind you of what to do (and what to avoid) for sales discovery meetings, ultimately developing habits that consistently lead to success.

What to Do

- ☐ Prepare for the meeting.

- ☐ Start the meeting on time.

- ☐ Make introductions and welcome everyone.

- ☐ Build rapport.

- ☐ Gain agreement on your meeting agenda.

- ☐ Focus on the prospect.

- ☐ Conduct a business-level conversation.

- ☐ Build credibility by validating research.

- ☐ Ask targeted questions.

- ☐ Actively listen.

- ☐ Pay attention to your prospects' body language.

- ☐ Be aware of your own nonverbal communication.

- ☐ Ask appropriate follow-up questions.

- [ ] Share relevant customer stories.

- [ ] Provide pertinent insights to add value.

- [ ] Use visuals appropriately.

- [ ] Collaborate with your prospects to determine if there's a fit (qualify in/qualify out).

- [ ] Make time in your meeting to discuss next steps.

- [ ] Collaborate with your prospects when identifying the next steps.

- [ ] Follow up on your promises after the meeting.

What Not to Do

- [ ] Don't be late.

- [ ] Don't jump directly into business discussions.

- [ ] Don't focus the conversation on you and your company.

- [ ] Don't lead with your product.

- [ ] Don't "show up and throw up" products or features.

- [ ] Don't automatically assume you know your prospect's business.

- [ ] Don't talk too much or speak too quickly.

- [ ] Don't ask so many questions that you irritate the prospect.

- [ ] Don't interrupt prospects when they are talking.

- ☐ Don't share irrelevant data as a way to make yourself look smart.

- ☐ Don't use technical jargon your prospects don't understand.

- ☐ Don't multitask during the meeting (checking phone/email, etc.).

- ☐ Don't allow "upspeak" to creep into your sentences.

- ☐ Don't use filler words.

- ☐ Don't bad-mouth the competition.

- ☐ Don't get defensive.

FOLLOWING BEST PRACTICES IN SALES CHECKLIST

Use this checklist to address gaps and ensure accountability for applying best practices as you navigate the sales process. Think carefully about each question and jot down any relevant notes before checking off each box.

Salesperson Name _____

Targeted Company _____

Prospect Name/Title _____

Prospecting

☐ Does this company align with your buyer profile? *(industry, company size, revenue, etc.)*

_____

☐ Does this person align with your buyer persona?

_____

☐ How are you integrating the three prospecting channels in a sequence to capture the attention of decision makers at this company? *(social, email, phone)*

_____

☐ How are you customizing the outreach based on your research?

_____

☐ Have you made actual contact with the prospect you are targeting?

_____

☐ Do you have any shared LinkedIn connections with this prospect? If so, could these people provide an introduction/ referral? If not, can you mention them in your prospecting communications?

_____

☐ What is your follow-up strategy? *(type, frequency)*

_____

☐ How many times have you followed up so far?

_____

Preparing for the Discovery Meeting

☐ Whom will you be meeting with?

_____

☐ What things stand out about the prospect, according to your research? *(facts for building rapport or engaging in business-level conversations)*

_____

☐ What initiatives/priorities/challenges are relevant to the prospect, based on the facts you've gathered?

_____

☐ What do you know about the organization's revenue growth/ decline in the past two quarters? *(assuming that information is public knowledge)*

_____

☐ What current/compelling events can be used to start a conversation with the prospect? *(recent news, press releases, financial summaries, earnings call transcripts)*

_____

☐ What are some industry trends you can leverage in discussions to add value?

_____

☐ How can you help the company/prospect, based on what you know so far?

_____

☐ Are there any clear indications the company would benefit from your solution?

_____

☐ How can you use the information you've gathered to build credibility and uncover opportunities in the discovery meeting?

_____

Maximizing Your Impact at the Meeting

☐ What steps can you take to make a positive first impression?

_____

☐ How can you build rapport with the prospect from the beginning?

_____

☐ What questions can you use to conduct a business-level conversation?

_____

☐ How will you remind yourself to listen actively during the discussions?

_____

☐ How can you manage the messages sent by your verbal *and* nonverbal communication?

_____

☐ How can you position yourself as a partner in solving the prospect's problems or achieving the prospect's objectives?

_____

☐ How will you strategically use visuals during the meeting?

_____

☐ What is your plan at the end of the meeting to confirm next steps?

_____

Qualifying the Opportunity

☐ Based on your discovery conversation, does the prospect's organization match your buyer profile?

_____

☐ Based on your discovery conversation, does the prospect match your buyer persona?

_____

☐ What are the company's initiatives and challenges?

_____

- [ ] What's the impact if the company does *not* address the challenges?

  _____

- [ ] What type of questions can you ask to qualify the opportunity?

  _____

- [ ] What does success look like for the company?

  _____

- [ ] Does your solution/product solve a business problem for this prospect?

  _____

- [ ] Does the prospect see the value in what you are offering?

  _____

- [ ] What is the timeline for the prospect to achieve the pertinent objectives?

  _____

- [ ] Can you deliver on the prospect's objectives within the specified time frame?

  _____

- [ ] Do you detect signs of interest in buying? *(responding to your emails, inviting others to the meeting, etc.)*

  _____

- [ ] Who are your competitors for this account?

  _____

☐ What is the role of the prospect in making a final decision? *(coach, champion, budget holder, etc.)*

_____

☐ Do you know the decision-making process inside the company and the roles of any additional people you're meeting?

_____

☐ Does the company have the budget available? Or can they reallocate funds to be able to afford your solution?

_____

☐ Is there a compelling event that increases the sense of urgency for purchasing your solution? *(data breach, recent competitive product launch, new compliance regulations, etc.)*

_____

☐ Is this a qualified opportunity? Why or why not?

_____

Taking Next Steps

☐ How can you most effectively follow up with the prospect after the meeting?

_____

☐ How can you detect a sense of urgency or a slowdown with the prospect?

_____

☐ What actions should come next to keep the deal moving forward?

_____

DISCOVERY MEETING ORGANIZER

Use this template before and during each sales discovery meeting. Besides helping you prepare, it will guide you to cover the essential topics and give you a simple way to organize your notes.

Company Name _____

Primary Contact _____

Date/Location of Meeting _____

Agenda Received/Confirmed _____

Setting the Stage

Attendee Name	Role/ Responsibilities	Rapport-Building Opportunities

Conducting a
Business-Level Conversation

Top Initiatives	Top Challenges	Desired Outcomes	Impact of Status Quo

Actively Listening

Questions Asked by the Prospect	Answers Provided to the Prospect

Building Credibility

Relevant Insights Shared	Relevant Customer Stories Shared

Engaging Additional Stakeholders

Other Key Players	Relevant Information They Shared

Identifying Your Competitors

Other Vendors Being Considered	Reasons Why	Counterpoints

Qualifying In

Viable Opportunity (Circle One)	Criteria/Rationale
Yes or No	
Yes or No	
Yes or No	

Discussing Next Steps

Summary: Key Points	Next Steps (If Qualified)	Date of Next Meeting	New Stakeholders Involved

Following Up

Prospect Requests	Completed	Your Promises to the Prospect	Completed

COLLABORATIVE SELLING SUMMARY

Populate this template to help you maximize the benefits of the collaborative selling process. Share the document with your colleagues to keep everyone on the same page, and be sure to update it regularly.

Potential Account

Company Name _____

Address _____

Website _____

Prospect Name (Primary Contact) _____

Internal Team Members

Name	Title	Role in the Sales Process	Responsibilities in the Meeting

Prospect Team Members

Key Player	Title	Role in the Sales Process	Supporter, Adversary, or Neutral	Past Relationship with Prospect

Prospect Team Profiles

Name	Personality Type	Communication Style	Words That Resonate with Them

Prospect Outlook

Current Initiatives or Priorities	Current Challenges or Pain Points

Prospect Requirements

Describe needs and parameters involved in determining a solution.

Compelling Event

Describe specific circumstances.

Competitors Being Considered

Company Name/ Solutions	Advantages	Disadvantages

Proposed Solution

Products/Services	Potential Deal Size

Results

Final Outcome _____

Target Closing Date _____

Additional Notes _____

DEBRIEFING SESSION GUIDE

Use this template as part of the debriefing session with your internal team members once a decision has been made by the prospect—win or lose. The information collected will help you evaluate the sales process, pinpointing both strengths and opportunities for improvement.

Account Name

Company Name	Primary Contact Person	Win or Loss

Internal Team Members

Name	Title	Role in the Sales Process

Prospect/Customer Team Members

Name	Title	Role in the Sales Process

Strengths

Describe areas/roles that provided an advantage during the sales process.

Opportunities for Improvement

Targeted Areas of Concern	Action Items to Facilitate Change	Lead/ Owner	Timeline

Outcome Evaluation

Complete the appropriate table.

Deal Won

Top Three Reasons for Winning	Competitors Involved	Potential Risk Factors Avoided	Strategies to Mitigate Risk Moving Forward

Deal Lost

Prospect Choice: Competitor's Solution or Status Quo	Top Three Reasons We Lost	Different Approaches That Might Have Changed the Outcome

Key Lessons Learned _____

_____

_____

_____

SALES METHODOLOGIES TO KNOW

Some sellers have mixed feelings about sales methodologies—not because they aren't effective. They are! But we've all heard stories about new leaders coming in and implementing their favorite versions. When they leave, those "flavor of the month" methodologies fizzle out. In comes another leader . . . and here we go again.

Aside from that, I want to emphasize that sales methodologies *really do work*. They have a purpose. There are many benefits to giving your sales process and message some structure, especially when teams commit to sticking with it.

Research by Gong validated the importance of using a formula and found that consistency in sales execution across the board is a common characteristic of top-performing sales organizations.[1] In fact, companies with a formal sales methodology produce more revenue.[2]

Chances are, you will eventually work for an organization that employs a specific sales methodology. Knowing some of the basics will help you get on board faster. Following are quick descriptions of some you've probably heard of, along with resources you can tap for more information. Please note that I don't endorse any particular methodology, I'm simply presenting these in alphabetical order.

Challenger Sales Model

This model emerged after an extensive study that analyzed thousands of sales reps in different industries.[3] The researchers used the data collected to identify distinct types of sellers and found that one in particular—the Challenger—consistently delivered high performance. Some organizations actively work to create sales teams that embody the characteristics of the Challenger:

- Educating potential buyers about what they're seeing in the industry

- Providing unique insights for prospects

- Tailoring messages to prospects' specific needs

- Challenging customers' ways of thinking, when appropriate[4]

Resource: Book

The Challenger Sale: Taking Control of the Customer Conversation by Matthew Dixon and Brent Adamson

Command of the Sale®

This methodology guides organizations to better equip their sales reps for qualifying opportunities, moving the process forward, and closing deals.[5] According to HubSpot, this approach involves selling with a sense of urgency, a degree of boldness, and extraordinary situational awareness.[6]

Resource: Website

https://www.forcemanagement.com/

Customer-Centric Selling

This model is designed to keep sales reps laser-focused on the needs of their potential customers. Organizations that choose this approach encourage salespeople to target decision makers rather than users, empowering them to buy instead of trying to convince them.[7] They also emphasize creating conversations around specific situations, asking relevant questions, and following the buyer's timeline.[8]

Resource: Book

CustomerCentric Selling (2nd ed.) by Michael T. Bosworth, John R. Holland, and Frank Visgatis

MEDDIC

This qualification-process approach (and all its variations) encourages sales reps to ask themselves and their prospects questions around **m**etrics, **e**conomics, **d**ecision criteria, **d**ecision processes, **i**dentified pain points, and **c**hampions.[9] Created in the 1990s, this model has evolved to include MEDDICC (which also considers competition) and MEDDPIC (which also considers paperwork).

Resource: Book

MEDDICC: The Ultimate Guide to Staying One Step Ahead in the Complex Sale by Andy Whyte[10]

SPIN Selling

SPIN Selling is a sales methodology that breaks the process into four categories: **s**ituation (gathering facts), **p**roblem (understanding the prospects' pain), **i**mplications (identifying the consequences of the pain), **n**eed payoff (evaluating the urgency of problem solving).[11] Originally introduced in 1988, this approach has been used in complex deals for decades.[12]

Resource: Book

SPIN Selling by Neil Rackham[13]

Exercise Answer Key

1. **How can Lydia build rapport with Roger to pave the way for a professional relationship?**

   - Lydia could bring up the topic of skydiving, asking about Roger's experiences and sharing the story of her recent jump.

2. **How can Lydia incorporate her research from Google and LinkedIn to improve the quality of the discovery meeting?**

   - Lydia can compassionately ask about the recent data breach, including details about the downtime, data loss, and costs. That line of questioning would focus on the effects of those events in terms of operations and profitability. The discussion can also help her uncover statistics about the bank's overall frequency of IT downtime, as well as the typical protocol for restoring functionality and information.

- Lydia can segue from that topic to inquire about the current technology situation—existing systems, any new initiatives established, changes made since the event, and solutions being considered.

- Lydia can provide some insights about the IT industry's latest advances in backup/recovery and cybersecurity best practices specifically designed for financial institutions. She may also share a story about another bank that faced similar issues and explain how her company created a customized solution that resulted in zero downtime and data loss over the past three years.

- Lydia can extend the discussion to include the pending acquisition mentioned by the CEO in the earnings call transcript, asking about any preliminary plans to merge and streamline the IT systems of the two organizations. She can mention the connection between data backup and digital transformation, referencing the LinkedIn article Roger had commented on. That will open the door for Lydia to share her insights on that topic and describe how her company partners with organizations throughout their digital transformation journeys.

3. **How can Lydia leverage the information about Roger shared by Darnell to make a greater impact?**

   - Appealing to Roger's preference for organization, Lydia can make sure her agenda is concise and focused with a logical structure. She can present information with objectivity and use analytical data to support key points.

- After listening carefully to Roger, she can ask thoughtful follow-up questions that demonstrate her grasp of the situation while pushing him to expand his thinking about alternative solutions.

INTERACTIVE EXERCISE 2: DURING THE SALE

1. **What is Lorenzo's first impression of Jerry?** *(timing, attire, attitude)*

   - Jerry's tardiness might be perceived as disrespectful, as well as an indication he is overwhelmed and overworked, and doesn't manage his time well.

   - Jerry's casual look can signal that this meeting wasn't important enough for him to comb his hair and present a professional image.

   - Lorenzo may perceive Jerry as being overwhelmed, especially given the way he started the meeting late, looked a bit disheveled, and appeared rushed. Jerry may have also seemed somewhat self-centered since he focused on his own questions and products rather than on the customer's needs.

2. **What mistakes did Jerry make when starting the meeting?**

   - Jerry neglected to conduct introductions. There were four additional people on the call from Lorenzo's team, and Jerry didn't know their names or roles in the sales process.

- Jerry didn't have an agenda. Lorenzo and the team didn't know the purpose or desired outcome of the meeting.

- Jerry didn't take time to build rapport and connect with his audience. His lack of preparation was evident from the beginning of the meeting.

3. **What changes can Jerry make to improve the quality of the discovery conversation?**

- Work to uncover Lorenzo's initiatives and challenges.

- Validate his research by asking targeted, strategic questions that he can't answer with a basic Google search.

- Actively listen and pay attention to nonverbal communications.

- Engage in dialogue instead of making it feel like an interrogation.

- Share relevant insights and customer stories that would resonate with the audience.

- Focus on how the solution could help the customer achieve business outcomes rather than simply highlighting features and functions.

- Engage all the key players on the call, using their names.

4. **What should Jerry have noticed about Lorenzo's body language?**

- Lorenzo was showing clear signs of frustration by sighing deeply, checking his watch, crossing his arms, and furrowing his brow. He felt like Jerry was wasting his time and not listening to him.

5. **What would you have done differently to end the meeting?**

- Summarize the information shared by Lorenzo and confirm everyone's understanding of the conversation is accurate.

- Intentionally reserve time to discuss next steps rather than making that feel like an afterthought.

- Collaborate with Lorenzo and his team to confirm action items, as well as roles and responsibilities, and potentially agree on a time for a follow-up meeting.

- Recognize that the end of the meeting—the ultimate outcome—is determined by the quality of advance preparation and the use of best practices during the meeting.

INTERACTIVE EXERCISE 3: AFTER THE SALE

1. **How should Maria structure the meeting with Liam to help avoid any hitches with the onboarding process?**

- Reconfirm the internal process with Liam for POs and SOWs to establish a general timeline for moving forward.

- Check to see if the company has specific SOW templates that should be used.

- Share with Liam the typical next steps based on her experience and describe what to expect.

- Advise Liam to confirm those steps with his internal resources since he is new to the role.

- Check with Liam to find out if he (or others involved in the approval process) will be out of the office in the next few weeks, which could impact the projected timeline.

2. **What best practices should Maria follow in handing off the new account to her internal team?**

- Provide relevant, concise information that will set up the internal team for successful implementation:

  - Detailed scope of the engagement as agreed upon in the final SOW

  - Any components of the MSA and other paperwork relevant to the team

  - Goals, initiatives, and expectations of the buyer's organization that need to remain the primary focus

  - Metrics that will be used to define success

  - Bios of key players for the customer, including roles, responsibilities, contact information, and communication preferences

  - Outline of the onboarding process (installations, training, development of support teams, or additional discussions)

- Clarify roles, expectations, and rules of engagement for internal team members.

- Identify strategies to keep the process moving forward despite upcoming vacation plans among team members.

- Introduce internal team members to the appropriate customer contacts to help facilitate a seamless handoff.

3. **How can Maria deepen and nurture the account relationship over time?**

- Remain in close contact with Liam to learn about any new initiatives or challenges with his business.

- Stay connected with the internal team to have consistent awareness of the account status.

- Ensure prompt delivery on promises made.

- Set up quarterly reviews with Liam to review progress and results.

- Continue to add value and provide relevant insights to Liam.

- Identify potential expansion opportunities with Liam and other departments across the organization.

- Ask for referrals (and potentially introductions) when the time is appropriate.

Notes

Chapter 1

1. Gartner, *Customer Centricity*, accessed February 14, 2023, https://www.gartner
   .com/en/marketing/glossary/customer-centricity.

Chapter 2

1. Salesforce, State of Sales, 3rd ed., accessed October 6, 2022, https://c1.sfdcstatic
   .com/content/dam/web/en_us/www/documents/reports/sales/state-of
   -sales-3rd-ed.pdf.
2. "Sales Turnover Statistics You Need to Know," *Xactly* (blog), August 24, 2021,
   https://www.xactlycorp.com/blog/sales-turnover-statistics.
3. Thomas F. Mahan et al., "2020 Retention Report: Trends, Reasons & Wake Up
   Call," Work Institute, accessed October 6, 2022, https://info.workinstitute.com
   /hubfs/2020%20Retention%20Report/Work%20Institutes%202020%20
   Retention%20Report.pdf.
4. Dominic Distel, Eric Hannon, Moritz Krause, and Alexander Krieg, "Finding the
   sweet spot in product-portfolio management," McKinsey & Company, December 4, 2020, https://www.mckinsey.com/business-functions/operations/our
   -insights/finding-the-sweet-spot-in-product-portfolio-management.
5. Ibid.
6. InsideSales Team, "How Much Do Companies Spend on Sales Technology Systems?," *InsideSales* (blog), September 18, 2017, https://www.insidesales.com
   /state-sales-2017-sales-technology-systems/.
7. LinkedIn State of Sales Report 2021: United States and Canada Edition, LinkedIn,
   accessed November 28, 2022, https://business.linkedin.com/sales-solutions
   /b2b-sales-strategy-guides/the-state-of-sales-2021-report.
8. Lisa Donchak, Julia McClatch, and Jennifer Stanley, "The future of B2B sales
   is hybrid," McKinsey & Company, April 27, 2022, https://www.mckinsey.com
   /capabilities/growth-marketing-and-sales/our-insights/the-future-of-b2b
   -sales-is-hybrid.

9. Ibid.

10. Arnau Bages-Amat, Liz Harrison, Dennis Spillecke, and Jennifer Stanley, "These eight charts show how COVID-19 has changed B2B sales forever," McKinsey & Company, October 14, 2020, https://www.mckinsey.com/business-functions /growth-marketing-and-sales/our-insights/these-eight-charts-show-how -covid-19-has-changed-b2b-sales-forever.

11. Ibid.

12. Ibid.

13. Donchak, McClatch, and Stanley, "The future of B2B," McKinsey & Company.

14. Brent Adamson, "Sensemaking for Sales," *Harvard Business Review*, January/ February 2022, https://hbr.org/2022/01/sensemaking-for-sales.

Chapter 3

1. Prabhakant Sinha, Arun Shastri, and Sally E. Lorimer, "5 Skills Every Salesperson Needs to Succeed," *Harvard Business Review*, September 19, 2022, https://hbr .org/2022/09/5-skills-every-salesperson-needs-to-succeed.

2. Ibid.

3. Dr. Tasha Eurich, "What Self-Awareness Really Is (and How to Cultivate It)," *Harvard Business Review*, January 4, 2018, https://hbr.org/2018/01/what-self -awareness-really-is-and-how-to-cultivate-it; Dr. Tasha Eurich, "Working with People Who Aren't Self-Aware," *Harvard Business Review*, October 19, 2018, https://hbr.org/2018/10/working-with-people-who-arent-self-aware.

4. Ibid.

5. Ibid.

6. Dr. Tasha Eurich, "The Science of Self Awareness for Salespeople," YouTube video, posted by Salesman.org, November 17, 2017, https://www.salesman .org/354-science-self-awareness-leads-sales-success-dr-tasha-eurich/; Erich C. Dierdorff and Robert S. Rubin, "Research: We're Not Very Self-Aware, Especially at Work," *Harvard Business Review*, March 12, 2015, https://hbr.org/2015/03 /research-were-not-very-self-aware-especially-at-work.

7. Eurich, "The Science of Self Awareness for Salespeople," https://www.salesman .org/354-science-self-awareness-leads-sales-success-dr-tasha-eurich/.

8. David Zes and Dana Landis, "A Better Return on Self-Awareness," *Briefings Magazine*, https://www.kornferry.com/insights/briefings-magazine/issue-17/better -return-self-awareness.

9. Eurich, "The Science of Self Awareness for Salespeople," https://www.salesman .org/354-science-self-awareness-leads-sales-success-dr-tasha-eurich/.

Chapter 4

1. Rana Salman, "Selling to the C-Suite: A Conversation with Shawn Taylor, Executive at Maverick Distribution Company," *LinkedIn* (blog), June 22, 2021, https://www.linkedin.com/pulse/selling-c-suite-conversation-shawn-taylor -executive-salman-ph-d-/.
2. Salesforce, State of the Connected Customer, 2nd ed., accessed October 7, 2022, https://www.salesforce.com/content/dam/web/en_gb/www/datasheets/state -of-the-connected-customer-report-second-edition2018.pdf.

Chapter 5

1. Rupal Bhandari, "Social Media Best Practices for B2B Businesses," *Gartner*, October 5, 2020, https://www.gartner.com/en/digital-markets/insights/social-media -best-practices-for-b2b-businesses-.
2. Mary Shea, "Keynote: The Future of Sales Enablement Is The C-Suite—Soirée, Boston," *Sales EnablementPro* (blog), June 11, 2019, https://salesenablement.pro /expertise/keynote-the-future-of-sales-enablement-is-the-c-suite-soiree-boston/.
3. G2 and Heinz Marketing, *The Impact of Reviews on B2B Buyers and Sellers: 2018 Benchmark Report*, accessed October 7, 2022, https://sell.g2.com/hubfs/Sell%20 Microsite%20Files/The%20Impact%20of%20Reviews%20on%20B2B%20-% 20Report.pdf.
4. Caroline Robertson, "A Social Take on Social Selling," *Forrester* (blog), April 11, 20128, https://www.forrester.com/blogs/a-social-take-on-social-selling/.
5. "Create an Effective Sales Profile on LinkedIn," LinkedIn, accessed October 7, 2022, https://business.linkedin.com/sales-solutions/resources/create-an -effective-sales-profile.
6. Mike Lieberman, "10 Stats About Inbound Marketing That Will Make Your Jaw Drop," *Insiders* (blog), HubSpot, January 20, 2014, updated February 18, 2020, https://blog.hubspot.com/insiders/inbound-marketing-stats.
7. LinkedIn Sales Solutions, "Effective Sales Profile," LinkedIn, https://business .linkedin.com/sales-solutions/resources/create-an-effective-sales-profile.
8. LinkedIn Marketing Solutions, "Reach an audience of 850M+ business professionals," LinkedIn, accessed October 7, 2022, https://business.linkedin.com /marketing-solutions/audience.

9. Aaron Bronzan, "Simple steps to a complete LinkedIn Profile," *LinkedIn* (blog), February 14, 2012, https://blog.linkedin.com/2012/02/14/profile-completeness.

10. Lydia Abbot, "10 Tips for Taking a Professional LinkedIn Profile Photo," *LinkedIn* (blog), April 19, 2022, https://www.linkedin.com/business/talent/blog/product-tips/tips-for-picking-the-right-linkedin-profile-picture.

11. LinkedIn Sales Solutions, "Effective Sales Profile," LinkedIn, Step 3, https://business.linkedin.com/sales-solutions/resources/create-an-effective-sales-profile#step3.

12. LinkedIn Sales Solutions Learning Center, "10 Steps to Optimize your Profile," LinkedIn video, accessed October 7, 2022, https://training.sales.linkedin.com/linkedin-profile-establish-your-professional-brand-empty/510962.

13. "LinkedIn Algorithm Report: Let's Talk with Richard van der Blom," YouTube video, posted by "Xavier Degraux," October 1, 2021, https://www.youtube.com/watch?v=7EvwEa_6cjQ.

14. Robert Cialdini, *Influence: Science and Practice*, 5th ed., performed by Lloyd James, Audible, 2012. Audiobook, Chapter 5.

Chapter 6

1. Matthew Cook, "14 Effective Sales Prospecting Techniques You Should Be Using, According to the Data," *Hubspot* (blog), January 18, 2023, accessed February 16, 2022, https://blog.hubspot.com/sales/effective-sales-prospecting-techniques-you-should-be-using.

2. Hans-Georg Wolff and Klaus Moser, "Effects of networking on career success: a longitudinal study," *Journal of Applied Psychology* 94, no.1 (2009): 196–206. doi:10.1037/a0013350, 202.

3. Marissa King and Balázs Kovács, "Research: We're Losing Touch with Our Networks," *Harvard Business Review*, February 12, 2021, https://hbr.org/2021/02/research-were-losing-touch-with-our-networks.

4. Kathleen Schaub, "Social Buying Meets Social Selling: How Trusted Networks Improve the Purchase Experience" (white paper), April 7, 2014, https://business.linkedin.com/content/dam/business/sales-solutions/global/en_US/c/pdfs/idc-wp-247829.pdf.

5. Rana Salman, "Selling to the C-Suite: A Conversation with Chris Townsend, CRO at CivicPlus," *LinkedIn* (blog), August 17, 2021, https://www.linkedin.com/pulse/selling-c-suite-conversation-chris-townsend-cro-rana-salman-ph-d-/.

6. Sara Howshar, "The Ultimate Guide to Cold Calling in 2022," *Chorus* (blog), Zoominfo, January 4, 2022, https://www.chorus.ai/blog/the-ultimate-guide-to-cold-calling.

7. Ibid.

8. Ibid.

9. Ibid.

10. Jenny Keohane, "The Best Sales Cadence Based on 33 Million Emails," *Yesware* (blog), May 3, 2022, https://www.yesware.com/blog/sales-cadence/.

11. "LinkedIn State of Sales Report 2022: United States and Canada Edition," LinkedIn, accessed October 7, 2022, https://business.linkedin.com/sales-solutions/b2b-sales-strategy-guides/linkedin-state-of-sales-report-2022.

12. Rana Salman, "Part I—Selling to the C-Suite: A Conversation with Ash Shehata, SVP, CIO at AHMC Healthcare Inc.," *LinkedIn* (blog), May 11, 2021, https://www.linkedin.com/pulse/part-iselling-c-suite-conversation-ash-shehata-svp-rana-salman-ph-d-/.

13. Mary Siewierska, "Cold Email Statistics Based on Sending Over 20M Cold Emails," *Woodpecker* (blog), updated January 10, 2022, https://woodpecker.co/blog/cold-email-statistics/.

14. Devin Reed, "This (surprising) cold email CTA will help you book A LOT more meetings," *Gong* (blog), May 27, 2020, https://www.gong.io/blog/this-surprising-cold-email-cta-will-help-you-book-a-lot-more-meetings/.

15. Chris Orlob, "Cold Calling Tips: 17 Proven Techniques to Master Your Cold Calls," *Gong* (blog), May 2, 2018, https://www.gong.io/blog/cold-calling-tips/.

16. Hang Wu et al., "Decoding subject's own name in the primary auditory cortex." *Human Brain Mapping*, Epub December 27, 2022, doi:10.1002/hbm.26186.

17. Dr. W. Staffen et al., "Selective brain activity in response to one's own name in the persistent vegetative state," *Journal of Neurology, Neurosurgery, and Psychiatry* 77, no. 12 (2006): 1383–1384, doi:10.1136/jnnp.2006.095166.

18. Ellen Langer, Arthur Blank, and Benzion Chanowitz, "The Mindlessness of Ostensibly Thoughtful Action: The Role of 'Placebic' Information in Interpersonal Interaction," *Journal of Personality and Social Psychology* 36, no. 6 (1978): 635–642, https://jamesclear.com/wp-content/uploads/2015/03/copy-machine-study-ellen-langer.pdf.

19. Ibid.

20. Orlob, "Cold Calling Tips," https://www.gong.io/blog/cold-calling-tips/.

21. Sara Howshar, "The Ultimate Guide to Cold Calling in 2022," *Chorus* (blog), Zoominfo, January 4, 2022, https://www.chorus.ai/blog/the-ultimate-guide-to-cold-calling.

22. Alan S. Cowen et al., "Mapping 24 emotions conveyed by brief human vocalization," *American Psychologist* 74, no. 6 (2019): 698–712, doi:10.1037/amp0000399.

23. Steven Macdonald, "How to Write a Follow Up Email (with 7 Examples, Backed by Research," *Superoffice* (blog), updated August 16, 2022, https://www.superoffice.com/blog/follow-up-email/.

24. Lisa Ross, "The Importance of Sale Follow Ups—Statistics and Trends," *Invesp* (blog), accessed October 7, 2022, https://www.invespcro.com/blog/sale-follow-ups/.

25. Zendesk, "The business impact of customer service on customer lifetime value," *Zendesk* (blog), published April 8, 2013, updated October 6, 2020, https://www.zendesk.com/blog/customer-service-and-lifetime-customer-value/.

26. Dave Elkington and James Oldroyd, *The InsideSales.com/MIT Lead Response Management Study*, October 16, 2007, https://cdn2.hubspot.net/hub/25649/file-13535879-pdf/docs/mit_study.pdf.

27. Dave Gerhardt, "Is Your Lead Management Leaking? We Tested 433 Companies," *Drift* (blog), February 27, 2017, https://www.drift.com/blog/lead-response-survey/.

Chapter 7

1. "Altify Knowledge Study Finds 74 Percent of Sellers Increase Win Rates with Account Planning," Altify, October 27, 2016, https://uplandsoftware.com/altify/resources/press-release/altify-knowledge-study-finds-74-percent-sellers-increase-win-rates-account-planning/.

2. LinkedIn, The LinkedIn State of Sales Report 2020: United States Edition, accessed October 7, 2022, 13, https://business.linkedin.com/content/dam/me/business/en-us/sales-solutions/resources/pdfs/state-of-sales_pocketguide_r11_v2.pdf.

3. Rana Salman, "Selling to the C-Suite: A Conversation with Scott Collison, President, and CEO at Personify Corp," *LinkedIn* (blog), April 20, 2021, https://www.linkedin.com/pulse/selling-c-suite-conversation-scott-collison-president-salman-ph-d-/.

4. Rana Salman, "From Sales to President to Vice-Chairman: What We Can All Learn from Tom Mendoza," *LinkedIn* (blog), July 24, 2019, https://www.linkedin.com/pulse/from-sales-president-vice-chairman-what-we-can-all-rana-salman-ph-d-/.

Chapter 8

1. Janine Willis and Alexander Todorov, "First Impressions: Making Your Mind After a 100-Ms Exposure to a Face," *Psychological Science* 17, no. 7 (July 2006): 592–598, https://doi.org/10.1111/j.1467-9280.2006.01750.x.

2. Laura Paige Naumann et al., "Personality judgments based on physical appearance," *Personality and Social Psychology Bulletin* 35, no. 12 (September 2009): 1661–1671; Joana Akweley Adotey, Ninette A. Pongo, and Elizabeth Obinnim, "The Relationship Between Clothes and First Impressions: Benefits and Adverse Effects on the Individual," *International Journal of Innovative Research and Advanced Studies* 3, no. 12 (November 2016): 229–234; Amanda Reid, Vince Lancuba, and Bridget Morrow, "Clothing Style and Formation of First Impressions," *Perceptual and Motor Skills* 84, no. 1 (February 1997): 237–238, doi:10.2466/pms.1997.84.1.237.

3. Lawrence Ian Reed, Rachel Stratton, and Jessica D. Rambeas, "Face Value and Cheap Talk: How Smiles Can Increase or Decrease the Credibility of Our Words," *Evolutionary Psychology* (October–December 2018), doi:10.1177/14747 04918814400.

4. S. M. Thierry, A. C. Twele, and C. J. Mondloch, "Mandatory First Impressions: Happy Expressions Increase Trustworthiness Ratings of Subsequent Neutral Images," *Perception* 50, no. 2 (February 2021): 103–115, doi:10.1177/0301006620987205.

5. Heike Jacob et al., "Effects of Emotional Intelligence on the Impression of Irony Created by the Mismatch Between Verbal and Nonverbal Cues," *PLoS ONE* 11, no. 10 (October 2016), https://doi.org/10.1371/journal.pone.0163211.

6. Geoffrey Beattie and Laura Sale, "Do metaphoric gestures influence how a message is perceived? The effects of metaphoric gesture-speech matches and mismatches on semantic communication and social judgment," *Semiotica* 2012, no. 192 (2012): 77–98, https://doi.org/10.1515/sem-2012-0067.

7. Kim Elsesser, "The Debate on Power Posing Continues: Here's Where We Stand," *Forbes* (blog), October 2, 2020, https://www.forbes.com/sites/kimelsesser /2020/10/02/the-debate-on-power-posing-continues-heres-where-we-stand /?sh=7ff06964202e.

8. John Maxwell, *Everyone Communicates, Few Connect: What the Most Effective People Do Differently* (New York: HarperCollins Leadership, 2010), 65.

9. Lang Chen et al., "Positive Attitude Toward Math Supports Early Academic Success: Behavioral Evidence and Neurocognitive Mechanisms," *Psychological Science* 29, no. 3 (2018): 390–402, https://doi.org/10.1177/0956797617735528.

10. Ibid.

11. Carol S. Dweck, *Mindset: The New Psychology of Success* (New York: Ballantine Books, 2007); Dr. Travis Bradberry, "Here's why your attitude is more important than your intelligence," *World Economic Forum* (blog), August 9, 2017, https://www.weforum.org/agenda/2017/08/heres-why-your-attitude-is-more-important-than-your-intelligence/.

12. Salesforce, State of the Connected Customer, 2nd ed., accessed October 7, 2022, 10, https://www.salesforce.com/content/dam/web/en_gb/www/datasheets/state-of-the-connected-customer-report-second-edition2018.pdf.

13. Casey A. Klofstad et al., "Sounds like a winner: voice pitch influences perception of leadership capacity in both men and women," *Proceedings Biological Sciences* 279, no. 1738 (2012): 2698, doi:10.1098/rspb.2012.0311.

14. Ibid.

15. Anna Oleszkiewicz et al., "Voice-based assessments of trustworthiness, competence, and warmth in blind and sighted adults," *Psychonomic Bulletin & Review* 24 (2017): 865–862, https://doi.org/10.3758/s13423-016-1146-y.

16. Brent Adamson, "Sensemaking for Sales," *Harvard Business Review*, January/February 2022, https://hbr.org/2022/01/sensemaking-for-sales.

17. Ibid.

18. LinkedIn, Global State of Sales 2022, accessed October 7, 2022, https://business.linkedin.com/sales-solutions/the-state-of-sales-2022-report.

19. Salesforce, State of Sales, 3rd ed., accessed October 6, 2022, https://c1.sfdcstatic.com/content/dam/web/en_us/www/documents/reports/sales/state-of-sales-3rd-ed.pdf.

Chapter 9

1. Chris Orlob, "How to Hack Rapport Building In Sales with This New Data," *Gong* (blog), May 24, 2017, https://www.gong.io/blog/hack-rapport-building-in-sales/.

2. Evan DeFilippis et al., "Collaborating During Coronavirus: The Impact of COVID-19 on the Nature of Work," *Harvard Business School Organizational Behavior Unit Working Paper* No. 21-006, *Harvard Business School Strategy Unit Working Paper* No. 21-006 (July 16, 2020), http://dx.doi.org/10.2139/ssrn.3654470.

3. Karen Huang et al., "It Doesn't Hurt to Ask: Question-Asking Increases Liking," *Journal of Personality and Social Psychology* 113, no. 3 (2017): 430–452, https://doi.org/10.1037/pspi0000097.

4. Alison Wood Brooks and Leslie K. John, "The Surprising Power of Questions," *Harvard Business Review*, May/June 2018, https://hbr.org/2018/05/the-surprising-power-of-questions.

5. Ibid.

6. Shawn Parrotte, "Sales Discovery Call Blog Series: What Is Your Ideal Discovery Flow?," *Chorus by Zoominfo* (blog), November 7, 2018, https://www.chorus.ai/blog/sales-discovery-call-blog-series-what-is-your-ideal-discovery-flow.

7. Chris Orlob, "The Highest Converting Talk-to-Listen Ratio in Sales, Based on 25,537 Sales Calls," *Gong* (blog), November 17, 2016, https://www.gong.io/blog/talk-to-listen-conversion-ratio/.

8. Ibid.

9. Brooks and John, "Power of Questions," *Harvard Business Review*, https://hbr.org/2018/05/the-surprising-power-of-questions.

10. Rana Salman, "Top Sales Tips and Lessons Learned: Interview with a Global Sales Leader," *LinkedIn* (blog), August 29, 2019, https://www.linkedin.com/pulse/top-sales-tips-lessons-learned-interview-global-rana-salman-ph-d-/.

11. Millward Brown, "Using Neuroscience to Understand the Role of Direct Mail," Case Study, accessed October 7, 2022, https://static1.squarespace.com/static/58ee4bac414fb53d228c3532/t/5d30cff8e172f9000121e612/1563480057602/MillwardBrown_CaseStudy_Neuroscience.pdf.

12. Ibid.

Chapter 10

1. Gordon Bower and Michal Clark, "Narrative Stories as Mediators for Serial Learning," *Psychonomic Science* 15 (April 1969): 181–182, doi:10.3758/BF03332778.

2. Ibid.

3. Thu-Huong Ha, "What Happens in the Brain When We Hear Stories? Uri Hasson at TED2016," *TEDBlog*, February 18, 2016, https://blog.ted.com/what-happens-in-the-brain-when-we-hear-stories-uri-hasson-at-ted2016/; Wendy A. Suzuki et al., "Dialogues: The Science and Power of Storytelling," *Journal of Neuroscience* 38, no. 44 (2018): 9468–9470, doi:10.1523/JNEUROSCI.1942-18.2018.

Chapter 11

1. Chris Orlob, "The 12 Best Objection Handling Skills for Sales You'll Ever Read," *Gong* (blog), April 17, 2018, https://www.gong.io/blog/objection-handling-techniques/.

2. Salesforce, *State of the Connected Customer*, 5th ed., accessed October 7, 2022, https://www.salesforce.com/content/dam/web/en_us/www/documents/research/salesforce-state-of-the-connected-customer-fifth-ed.pdf.

3. Salesforce, *State of the Connected Customer*, 4th ed., accessed October 7, 2022, https://lg-static.techrepublic.com/direct/whitepapers/Salesforce_4th_Edition_State_of_Connected_Customer.pdf.

4. Salesforce, "Is Collaborative Selling the Answer to Increased Productivity and Pipeline?," *Salesforce blog*, July 31, 2017, https://www.salesforce.com/content/blogs/au/en/2017/07/is-collaborative-selling-the-answer-to-increased-productivity-an.html.

5. The Economist Intelligence Unit, *Communication barriers in the modern workplace*, accessed October 7, 2022, https://impact.economist.com/perspectives/sites/default/files/EIU_Lucidchart-Communication%20barriers%20in%20the%20modern%20workplace.pdf.

6. Summer Allen, "The Science of Gratitude" (white paper), May 2018, accessed October 7, 2022, https://ggsc.berkeley.edu/images/uploads/GGSC-JTF_White_Paper-Gratitude-FINAL.pdf.

Chapter 12

1. Daniel Mochon, "Single-Option Aversion," *Journal of Consumer Research* 40, no. 3 (2013): 555–566, https://doi.org/10.1086/671343.

2. Sheena S. Iyengar, and Mark R. Lepper, "When Choice Is Demotivating: Can One Desire Too Much of a Good Thing?," *Journal of Personality and Social Psychology* 79, no. 6 (2000): 995–1006, doi:10.1037//0022-3514.79.6.995.

3. C. Northcote Parkinson, "Parkinson's Law," *Economist*, November 19, 1955, https://www.economist.com/news/1955/11/19/parkinsons-law.

Chapter 13

1. Matthew Dixon and Brent Adamson, *The Challenger Sale: Taking Control of the Customer Conversation* (New York: Portfolio, 2011), 47.

2. Andy Fred Wali and Bright Chidugam Opara, "The Impact of Customer Appreciation Service on Customer Loyalty Patronage: Evidence from Nigeria Financial Sector," *European Journal of Business and Management* 5, no. 1 (2013), https://www.researchgate.net/publication/263620229_The_Impact_of_Customer_Appreciation

_Service_on_Customer_Loyalty_Patronage_Evidence_from_Nigeria_Financial _Sector.

3. Jeffrey Slater, "The Thank You Experiment," *LinkedIn* (blog), April 12, 2015, https://www.linkedin.com/pulse/thank-you-experiment-jeffrey-slater/.

4. Nick Toman, Brent Adamson, and Cristina Gomez, "The New Sales Imperative," *Harvard Business Review*, March/April 2017, https://hbr.org/2017/03/the-new -sales-imperative.

5. Gallup, *Guide to Customer Centricity: Analytics and Advice for B2B Leaders*, 2016, accessed October 7, 2022, https://clienteg.com/wp-content/uploads/2017/07 /Gallop-B2B-Customer-Centricity-Report.pdf.

6. Amy Gallo, "The Value of Keeping the Right Customers," *Harvard Business Review*, October 29, 2014, https://hbr.org/2014/10/the-value-of-keeping-the -right-customers.

Chapter 15

1. Gartner, *Why Accounts Aren't Growing, and What to Do About It*, 2019, accessed October 7, 2022, https://emtemp.gcom.cloud/ngw/globalassets/en/sales -service/documents/trends/why-accounts-arent-growing.pdf; Tim Stafford, "How Smart Account Management Boosts Sales Growth," *Gartner* (blog), November 14, 2017, https://www.gartner.com/smarterwithgartner/how-smart -account-management-boosts-sales-growth.

2. Gartner, *Why Accounts Aren't Growing*, https://emtemp.gcom.cloud/ngw /globalassets/en/sales-service/documents/trends/why-accounts-arent -growing.pdf.

3. Ibid.

4. Nielsen Insights, "Consumer Trust in Online, Social and Mobile Advertising Grows," Nielsen, April 2012, https://nielsen.com/insights/2012/consumer-trust -in-online-social-and-mobile-advertising-grows/.

5. John Hall, "The 5 Things All Great Salespeople Do," *Forbes* (blog), February 3, 2019, https://www.forbes.com/sites/johnhall/2019/02/03/the-5-things-all -great-salespeople-do/?sh=48078c931232.

Chapter 16

1. Mark Travers, "A Psychology Professor Explains the Best Way to Deal with Rejection," *Therapytips*, April 18, 2022, https://therapytips.org/interviews/a-psychology -professor-explains-the-best-way-to-deal-with-rejection.

2. Naomi I. Eisenberger, "The neural bases of social pain: Evidence for shared representations with physical pain," *Psychosomatic Medicine* 74, no. 2 (2012): 126–135, doi:10.1097/PSY.0b013e3182464dd1.
3. Rana Salman, "Tips to Crush It in Sales: Interview with an Amazing Sales Leader!," *LinkedIn* (blog), August 1, 2018, https://www.linkedin.com/pulse/tips -crush-sales-interview-amazing-leader-rana-salman-ph-d-/.

Chapter 17

1. Tim Clarke, Jeff Riseley, and Richard Harris, 2022 State of Mental Health in Sales Report, accessed December 5, 2022, https://saleshealthalliance.com/2022-state -of-mental-health-in-sales-report/.
2. Ibid.
3. "Research Findings: Burnout in the Sales Industry UNCrushed Survey," UNCrushed, October 8, 2019, https://www.uncrushed.org/content/2019/10/8 /research-findings-burnout-in-the-sales-industry-uncrushed-survey.

Sales Essentials Toolkit

1. Chris Orlob, "Consistency: The Unfair Advantage of Top-Notch Sales Organizations," *Gong* (blog), October 11, 2018, https://www.gong.io/blog/the-secret -behind-top-notch-sales-teams/.
2. Jason Jordan and Robert Kelly, "Companies with a Formal Sale Process Generate More Revenue," *Harvard Business Review*, January 21, 2015, https://hbr .org/2015/01/companies-with-a-formal-sales-process-generate-more-revenue.
3. Matthew Dixon and Brent Adamson, *The Challenger Sale: Taking Control of the Customer Conversation* (New York: Portfolio, 2011).
4. Ibid.
5. Force Management, *Command of the Sale*, accessed October 7, 2022, https:// cdn2.hubspot.net/hubfs/3334729/Product%20Sheet%20PDFs/FM%20 Command%20of%20the%20Sale.pdf?t=1498252885674.
6. Emma Brudner, "12 Best Sales Methodologies & Customer-Centric Selling Systems," *HubSpot* (blog), July 14, 2022, updated September 14, 2022, https://blog .hubspot.com/sales/6-popular-sales-methodologies-summarized.
7. Michael Bosworth, John Holland, and Frank Visgatis, *CustomerCentric Selling*, 2nd ed. (New York: McGraw-Hill, 2010).
8. Ibid.

9. "MEDDICC Sales Methodology and Practice," MEDDICC, accessed October 7, 2022, https://meddicc.com/meddic/.

10. Andy Whyte, *MEDDICC: The Ultimate Guide to Staying One Step Ahead in the Complex Sale* (Cambridgeshire, UK: MEDDICC Limited, 2020).

11. Aja Frost, "SPIN Selling: The Ultimate Guide," *HubSpot* (blog), June 9, 2022, updated July 26, 2022, https://blog.hubspot.com/sales/spin-selling-the-ultimate-guide.

12. "Neil Rackham," *Wikipedia*, last modified October 7, 2022, https://en.wikipedia.org/wiki/Neil_Rackham#SPIN_Selling.

13. Neil Rackham, *Spin Selling* (New York: McGraw-Hill, 1988).

Index

About the Author

Photo by Lifetouch

Rana Salman, MBA, PhD, is a recognized expert in the sales industry. Leveraging her successful background in marketing and enterprise-level B2B sales, she now partners with global organizations to help them strategically elevate the performance of their sales teams.

As founder of Salman Consulting, LLC, Rana supports her clients—midsize and Fortune 500 IT companies—by designing customized sales strategies, creating effective sales content, and developing high-impact training sessions delivered in person, through webinars, and on demand. She specializes in sales enablement that optimizes the end-to-end customer experience as a tool to build loyalty and increase revenue.

Rana is a cofounder of WiSE (Women in Sales Enablement), a robust networking group that connects female sales enablement professionals from around the globe to share ideas and learn from one another.

Rana was honored to be included on the list of Women Making an Impact in Enablement by Sales Enablement PRO (2022) and named one of the Top Female Sales Practitioners for Your Next Panel, Presentation, or Podcast by Sales Hacker (2021). She has been a guest speaker at a variety of high-profile events, including the Texas Conference for Women, Sales Enablement Society Conference, and Competitive Marketing Summit.

ABOUT SALMAN CONSULTING

Salman Consulting develops practical, targeted solutions to help sales teams build healthy pipelines, qualify opportunities, and close deals. The firm's offerings include:

- Analyzing sales strategies to determine gaps and identify opportunities for improvement

- Collaborating with sales, marketing, and enablement leaders to address those gaps

- Building and strengthening sales-enabled cultures to optimize the end-to-end customer experience from pre-sales to post-sales

- Delivering customized training in person, through virtual platforms, and on demand

- Providing unique sales content, coaching, and keynote presentations to improve sales effectiveness

• • •

For more information about Rana's availability for consulting, training, and speaking, please email her at rana.salman@salmanconsulting .com. You can also connect with her through LinkedIn at linkedin.com /in/ranasalman1 or visit her website at www.SalmanConsulting.com.